D1785183

AUDREY

CAROLE SANYAL (NÉE GLEAVE)

1938-2010

HER UNFINISHED AUTOBIOGRAPHY
AND TRIBUTES BY
HER FAMILY AND FRIENDS

Also by Audrey Sanyal:

Talavera: Tongued with Fire
Diadem Books, 2010
ISBN 978-1907294433

Naseby: This Phantom Ground
Diadem Books, 2010
ISBN 978-0955985270

Published by Memoirs

MEMOIRS
PUBLISHING

25 Market Place, Cirencester, Gloucestershire, GL7 2NX
info@memoirsbooks.co.uk www.memoirspublishing.com

Audrey Carole Sanyal (née Gleave): 1938-2010
Her unfinished autobiography and tributes by
her family and friends.

All Rights Reserved. Copyright © 2013 **Audrey Sanyal**

No part of this book may be reproduced or transmitted in any
form or by any means, graphic, electronic, or mechanical, including
photocopying, recording, taping or by any information storage or
retrieval system, without the permission in writing from
the copyright holder.

The right of Audrey Sanyal to be identified as the author of this work
has been asserted in accordance with the Copyright, Designs
and Patents Act 1988 sections 77 and 78.

The views expressed in this work are solely those of the author or
contributors and do not necessarily reflect the views of the publisher,
and the publisher hereby disclaims any responsibility for them.

ISBN: 978-1-909874-44-2

Acknowledgements

Audrey's family gratefully acknowledges the tributes by her friends—Norma Smyth, Wendy Humphries, Mary Stephenson and Jenny Grixti.

It would not have been possible to include the Section on the photos without the help of Harminder (Bob) Panesar.

The family is immensely grateful to him for his kindness.

INTRODUCTION

17 January 1959 changed my life!

I, Anupam Sanyal, from Calcutta (now called Kolkata), India was in the 2nd year of my PhD study at Sheffield University, England.

Saturday was the day when we had our weekly dances at the Students' Union. My friend Chung Sung Lee from Korea and I had planned to go for a dance. We had a choice; we could go to the City Dance Hall at Nether Edge where the entrance fee was 1 Shilling and 8 Pence. To go to the Union would cost 9 Pence! Although we could afford the difference, we tossed a coin. The Union won.

We made our way there.

I had a purpose (God had a bigger one!!) other than just a weekly something to pass the time. It was to find a partner at the Going Down Ball. This is the End of Term Dance where you had to have a partner, unlike the weekly dances where one could dance with any boy or girl. You could go to the Going Down Ball without a partner but then you would have to sit around and watch!

I thought I might meet a girl at this dance who I could take as my partner to this Going Down Ball before the Easter Break.

So Chung Sung and I went there and had one or two dances but didn't meet any girl that I felt like asking for the Going Down Ball. There were breaks in between dances. During one of these, I looked across the dance floor and I saw a blonde girl in blue and white striped frock talking to another girl. The blonde was stunningly beautiful and I wondered if I should ask her for the next dance when I could broach the subject. When the Band started playing, (yes Live Band, no Juke Box!), I took courage in my hand and went across and asked her if I could have the next dance. I wasn't sure if she was available and whether such a pretty girl would not have a man with her. But she said –"Yes, OK." So we started dancing. I was no good at it at all, which she must have realized quite soon. I had taken a few dancing lessons—Waltz, Quick Step and Rock & Roll, which didn't need much learning. These were all the dances I could do. During the course of this dance, when I managed to avoid trampling on her feet, she told me her name was Audrey and she was in the final year of her Teachers' Training Course at the University.

I mentioned the Going Down Ball and the date and asked her if she would be willing to be my Partner. She said, "I will think about it."

This was 17 January 1959. She was my partner at the Going Down Ball and was my wife for Forty-Nine Years, Five months and Twenty-Five days, when God suddenly took her away over an hour on the 31st October 2010!

We had known each other for nearly 52 years.

This is an account of her Life so that you might know her better.

When we were a middle- aged couple, I asked her several times to write her autobiography.

Her reply always was that she didn't like to write about people who were alive. I told her to write about the people who had passed away. Whether it was my pestering or she was in a writing mood, she did write about a small part of her life before she took to writing fiction, and had two historical novels published, and had begun to write the third to constitute a trilogy when she suddenly passed away.

So, here is her unfinished autobiography followed by memoirs provided by her friends and family.

Anupam Sanyal

TABLE OF CONTENTS

Chapter 1

Audrey's Autobiography

Layers for Medlars

by

Audrey Carole Sanyal

I

Whenever my mother returned from a shopping trip we would ask what she had in the basket, boxes or bags. Every time she would reply, 'Layers for Medlars.'

These words drove me crazy. I have never found out what they meant. If you ask what is in this book, all I can say is, 'Layers for Medlars.' May be exotic perfume wrapped in silk, or simply a pound of carrots—the fabric of interwoven lives.

There ought to be a book written about me; when I grow up I'll write one—but today seemed to be the right time to begin. Begin at the beginning and go right through to the end. The wonderland existence of childhood!

I was born on December 7th 1938.

My parents were Ernest and Zena Gleave.

My parents chose my first name but there are two versions as to who chose Carole. My cousin Dorothy maintains that as my birthday was near Christmas, she suggested Carole. The other version is that Dad's eldest sister Aunty Annie chose the name.

One of the earliest incidents, I can remember, is being wheeled in my pushchair surrounded by cushions. We entered into a marvellously smelly place full of rabbits in cages and flowers. There were huge shire horses with plaited tails. I think that it must have been the Annual Flower Show held by my Dad's factory. Although the main livelihood of the locals was in industry we seemed to have pursued fairly rural pastimes.

I remember my cot, which was pink. It was right next to my parents' bed and every night I held my Mum's hand until I fell asleep.

Does every generation think that people were kinder in the past? I have this rosy picture of a time when it was safe for small children of six or so to walk to school alone. On reflection this could be because all the most dangerous types were off doing what they did best, quite legitimately killing people, in the war?

I am standing against park railings that have not been ground up for the war effort. My hair appears quite golden, maybe on account of the poetic license of the tint of the photograph. I am wearing a pink dress and black shoes that fastened with cross straps and buttons. Just after this photo was taken the sirens sounded; my mother and father grabbed me and we all dashed back home.

This gilded image of me graced our piano for many years.

Did anyone ever go into shelters? Not where I lived. St Helens, my hometown, was lucky in that only one bomb was dropped on it. This was quite remarkable considering that it was a mere twelve miles from Liverpool and had many factories, all involved in war work. The sirens sounded and we would take refuge under the stairs. I still have the table we sat behind. It has crossed the Atlantic four times! It is one of those huge Victorian pieces with massive carved legs. Originally it had to be cranked apart to insert an extension.

A mattress was put on the floor behind this bulwark. I imagine that if a hit had been scored this article of furniture would have disintegrated and skewered us all! Our neighbours always came round to join us in the under stairs vigil. I would have been three at this time and I remember that the ghastly boy from next door beside, with whom, I would have to sleep, regularly wet the bed.

I adored my Mickey Mouse gas mask and would have worn it all day if given the chance. One of my earliest memories is sitting in front of the fire and seeing my dad come in wearing his Special Constable's uniform. It had one of those high collars, which looked so uncomfortable. All the factories were active twenty-four hours a day and nearly everyone worked twelve-hour shifts. My father would come home and then go on fire watch or patrol his beat. He had always wanted to be a policeman but they had some height restrictions. He could now fulfil his wish but how he had the energy to do all this amazes me.

If there was an idle moment, working on an allotment was almost mandatory. Any land lying fallow was turned over to the cultivation of edible crops. Ours was on land abutting our church. Many kinds of vegetables were cultivated. Peas, beans, potatoes, cauliflowers and cabbages. The enemy here was the caterpillar and I was employed in picking these pests from the cabbages and peas.

As my granny was there to look after me, my mother worked in an ammunitions factory. According to her this was a catharsis. Well, I am sure she never said, or thought 'catharsis', but it certainly was a revelation. I can never imagine that my mum had ever been a shrinking violet, yet apparently this had been so. While working in the factory she was chosen by her workmates to be their spokesperson. She found that she was capable of speaking to anyone and continued to do so for the rest of her life.

My granny and I would go through the park to meet my mum and her friends as they came home from work. They would link arms and come along the path, singing. Some of the most popular songs were 'You are my sunshine' and something I thought was

> Mersey dotes and Dozy dotes
> And little lamsy tivy
> A kiddly tivy too...

Later I found out that this was really:

> Mares eat oats and do eat oats
> And little lambs eat ivy.
> A kid'll eat ivy too, wouldn't you?

16

With my grandmother I attended the weekly church sewing meetings. I must have been a singularly well-behaved child as I was allowed to sift through the efforts that had been made for the Christmas Fayre. It was always a 'Fayre', never a 'Fair'—some quaint medieval concept? The items made for the sale were kept in what, to me, resembled a treasure chest. Beautiful embroidery and crochet work. I was also fascinated by the fact that the minister's wife always wore a crocheted beret, like a skullcap. It seemed to be a permanent fixture.

I started school when I was three. As we could not read we all had a symbol on the peg where we would hang our coat and the canvas bag in which were kept pencils and books. My symbol was an apple, maybe because its initial letter was also that of my name.

In the first class it was supposed to be a great treat to be given a ride on the rocking horse. I was terrified of this beast. Sitting on its back I seemed to be miles from the floor. We counted with shells. All the windows had brown sticky tape on them. We played shop with wax fruit. Every afternoon we slept on small camp beds.

On our road was a shop, which had been a greengrocer. In the corner of the window was a picture advertising Fyffe's bananas. I now know that these were Fifes Bananas, 'i' as in *sigh*, but we called them Fifi's—'i' as in *big*.

Does the obsession to speak 'correctly' still remain? We had our Lancastrian vowel sounds drummed out of us at grammar school. Bath (as in *hath*) became barth (as in *aha*) and we interminably 'dahnced' and 'prahnced' on the 'grahss'!

I occasionally see English films from the thirties. They speak with such strangulated accents. Did people ever really talk like this?

There is a tradition that the reclusive Hill Billies of Virginia speak with what was a sixteenth or seventeenth century English accent. "To be or not to be y'all!"

To return to the banana. My mother, whose favourite fruit this was, would look longingly into the distance. "That's a banana and when the war is over we will have all the bananas that we can eat." Years later I did receive one of these elusive objects. I was only allowed to take it to school providing that I shared it with my friends.

As I was the only child I was constantly being told to share things. Maybe because I was an only child I made, what came to be, long lasting friendships. We had a large family of uncles, aunts and cousins.

Books, which were very hard to acquire in wartime, were treasured possessions. Two of my favourites were *The World Atlas* and another geographical offering, *Around the World in Pictures*. The photographs were in black and white and indigenous people were doing quaint ethnic activities. Easy to scoff at this simplistic approach but it engendered a lifelong interest in other places and people.

The books of Enid Blyton also featured prominently. I still have some very dog-eared volumes. These are pre-noddy vintage: *The Happy Story Book*, *Eight o'clock Tales*, *The Caravan Family* and *The Magic Faraway Tree*. I especially enjoyed *The Magic Faraway Tree*. Children climb a tree and at the top there is always a new land. Some of the adventures were quite scary and the protagonists would have to make a quick exit. The 'Five' books, which I think were written later, involved four children and a dog going off by themselves and experiencing impossible adventures. How we longed to travel with our friends in a gypsy caravan, untrammelled by the presence of parents.

A development in the educational world of the early 80s was the theory that children want to read stories that mirror their own environment. My friends and I certainly never wanted to read such books. It was far preferable to imagine leaving by train, hockey sticks in hand, heading towards Summer Term at St Clare's. I still desperately want to discover a secret passage in an old inn in Rye!

My book about Jesus had to be handled very carefully as it had stand-up pictures. I was only allowed to get it out on very special occasions.

II

'You'd only have to whisper a hint to Time and
round goes the clock in an Instant.'

Church was the centre of our social life as well as spiritual. A congregational church had originally been started by a small group of local people who wanted a place of worship which was nearer than the mother church in town.

With such a wonderful rightness, services were held above

a stable. The horses, Dobbin and Shamrock, moved about below. These horses pulled milk floats. My mother said that they were taken away to France in the First World War never to return.

My mother Zena Beatrice was born in 1908. She was the child of the second marriage of both my grandmother and grandfather.

I heard tales of the terrible time my grandmother had with her first husband. Apparently he drank. His name was Foster. My grandmother never spoke of him or of the two children of this marriage who died of tuberculosis. I only heard this from my mother.

These two children, a boy and girl, were buried in a local churchyard. For some reason many years prior to the general trend to grass over small burial grounds, this particular church cleared most of the tombstones. Many times when we passed the building my mum would say that these two were buried somewhere there.

I think that granny's husband also died of tuberculosis. At that time the disease was usually fatal.

My grandmother was a midwife. In her old age she kept all her important documents in her nurse's bag. She was a woman with a career at a time when not many women were capable of earning their own livings.

Medical treatment had to be paid for. Most people were poor but among them there was a social stigma in accepting "charity".

In those days ladies wore quite voluminous long dresses. If my grandmother attended someone in dire need she would wear two sets of clothes so that one could be given to the patient but no one would know.

She was a pillar of the community. She sat on the board of something called 'Sunshine Babies'. I have no idea what this was. A charity for poor children?

She travelled into Liverpool to areas, where policemen feared to tread, to attend women in labour.

In my Granny's youth the Workhouse was an active institution. Everyone had a dread of ever going there. In her old age my grandmother said that she was never to be admitted to Whiston Hospital as in times long past it had been a Poor (Work) House.

My grandmother Mary Harriet married William Cheetham. He already had five children. My granny then had my Uncle Eric and my mother. She must have been in her early forties or late thirties as she died at the age of 86, when I was 11 years old.

In my very early years she was my constant companion. At this time she would have been in her early seventies. When at home she looked like a typical grandmother of a fairy tale, round and rosy with white hair. She always wore a pinafore over her dress. These were a special kind of pinny. I can feel the material now, thick silky cotton. My clearest memory is of a black pinafore, which was embroidered with small violets.

When she went out she took on the demeanour of Queen Mary!

She always wore thick silky stocking and shoes with pointed toes and the ubiquitous cross strap and buckle. In the distant future this would all be fashionable again.

She also had in her possession things called modesty vests. These were long, elaborately embroidered, triangles of material, which were placed in the strategic position if the cleavage of a dress was considered a little too risqué.

My granny taught me how to play cards and draughts.

I am sure that she told me many tales of her childhood but I only remember a few. Why didn't I ask her more about herself?

Her father was a gamekeeper i.e. a farm labourer on the Derby Estate. Whether it was the superior or less munificent occupation, his employment entitled him to a tied cottage and a quite abundant supply of food. An inherited tradition of four square meals, including a cooked supper was the norm in our house for many a long year.

I can still taste the rabbit pies she made. We received sausage meat from the USA; this too was made into pies. I naively thought that this delicious commodity would be available in the America of the 90s. I have scoured the shelves of many grocery stores without success.

A pear tree grew outside her bedroom window. The blossom filled the air in springtime and when the wind blew, the branches scraped against the panes, scaring her at night.

When we lived in London, a white blossom tree grew outside our bedroom window. If confined to bed there was a feeling of floating on a sea of blossom foam. This romantic image vanished with the storms, as the tree became unsafe and had to be cut down.

In America the blossom branches screech and chat away at night, and their pink blooms herald the spring.

If Mary Harriet or any of the family had to walk through the woods at night, they would carry a torch. Not the modern flashlight but a flaming torch. Apparently at certain times of the year the stags, which inhabited the forest, became dangerous and were only frightened away by fire. The grounds of this estate are now home to the far fiercer lions, which inhabit the Safari Park.

Having lived the rural life, my grandmother had the useful or unfortunate ability to kill animals. In our more urban setting this took the form of wringing chickens' necks and plucking their feathers. Vermins were dispatched by a hefty whack with a coal shovel!

For a short period during the war we kept two turkeys, fattening them up for Christmas. I have a feeling that this may have been a slightly illegal operation. Their names were Monty and Stalin and their home was the outside toilet at the end of the yard. We gave up the use of this facility and they had the sole occupation of the edifice. Feeding them was a messy and smelly job. I realize now that this was a rustic 'chore'. (Why do adults think that feeding poultry is a treat for small children?).

My Aunty Evelyn and Uncle Walter lived on Rainford

Road. Today I would consider this quite a short drive from the place where we lived. Then it seemed like a major expedition.

My Aunty Evelyn kept hens. The hens lived in a proper hen house. My Aunt thought that I loved to go and fetch eggs and feed the demons. I couldn't abide them. Their beady eyes seemed riveted on my chubby legs and their beaks poised for pecking. I must admit I never actually came under attack. My Uncle Walter stirred great vats of evil smelling porridgy stuff for them. He also fed blood to his vine. This sounds like the realm of Dracula but it must have been animal blood, which provided iron for the plant.

Their garden was divided into many sections. Beneath the dining room windows were banks of hydrangeas. Beyond them was an immaculate lawn of Bowling Green consistency, surrounded by banks of graduated flowers. Stocks, lupines, pansies, dahlias and many others stood to attention in height-regulated rows. I do not remember roses but there must have been some. A greenhouse for the bloodsucking vine, tomatoes, heat-loving flowers and cacti separated this very formal section from the vegetable garden.

Within this vegetable area were also many flowers; sweet peas grew along with their more prosaic green pea relatives. There was a crabapple tree. The fruit of this was so bitter but it was religiously harvested and made into crabapple jelly. Many dusty jars of this singularly inedible concoction graced the pantry shelves of relatives.

There was a further orchard with pear and apple trees. In this area daisies grew and blossom spattered the ground.

Again the assumption was that Audrey loved to brave the wasps and gather fruit! In later years when watching American films in which children on farms were always doing chores, I realized that I too had been a chore doer!

At the bottom of the garden was a wood. For me this was great place to explore but sometimes a little scary in the way that woods have about them. What lurked behind the trees? Rooks cawed and swooped. The wood behind our house in Ohio brought back memories of this.

We lived in a terraced house. There was a small garden at the front. Marigolds and lily of the valley were the predominant flowers. There was the inevitable privet hedge and stone wall surround, and a green gate from which a path led to a heavy green door. This was the door we locked and bolted at night but it was always left open during the day. The inner vestibule door had a bell but no lock at all. People were expected to ring, but the usual form of entry was a brief burst on the bell, followed by opening the door, then a shout of "It's only me" from whomever the 'me' might be.

We had a back yard. Along the edge of this my father had dug an area where every year the same kind of flowers and fruit were planted. Polyanthus and primroses. Nasturtiums and strawberries. A small area next to the washhouse was planted with hydrangeas and there was a wrought iron bench.

The washhouse contained what would now be collectors' items. Washday was an event when tempers would be frayed. I forget how the water was heated but it ended up in two tubs. A dolly tub and a rinsing tub. The dolly looked to me like cow's udders. It was a long pole at one end of which was a circle of short thick spars. The dolly was rotated so that the articles being washed were thoroughly cleaned. The washing was then transferred into the rinsing tub and the posser came into action. This was a kind of large colander at the end of a pole. It was lifted up and down to further agitate the clothes. After a good possing the clothes would be put through the mangle, which had very large wooden rollers, reminiscent of a medieval instrument of torture. A third tub received the drips. Finally everything was pegged out on the line. A prop was used to elevate the washing line. If I touched this I always got a splinter in my hand. Why wasn't it made from less splinter-prone wood?

An electric boiler with an attached mangle eventually superseded this antediluvian, back-breaking process. The whole operation was re-located to the back kitchen, which made life easier, but possing and dollying were still required.

My mother was all for progress and as soon as washing machines were available, she bought one. There was an electrically operated mangle on the first model. Clothes dried on the line or in bad weather on a clotheshorse in front of the fire. After this, the ritual of airing began. The airing cupboard was upstairs next to the water boiler and clothes could only be worn if they had been suitably aired. There was a rack arrangement, which hung from the ceiling, which also served as an airing venue. This was raised and lowered by a pulley.

The washhouse contained all kinds of tools. My father repaired his own shoes so that there was a cobbler's last and all the special knives required for cutting leather. The pervasive smell was one of leather and soap flakes. Our bikes were kept in there too.

The house next door had a lilac tree, the branches of which hung over our wall and gave off a perfume occasionally filtered through eau de turkey!

Monty and Stalin in all their glory were fattening up well. Of course by the time Christmas rolled around they had assumed the role of pets and no way could any of us, not even Granny, approve that we kill or eat them. On the other hand we could not keep two adult turkeys forever. They were taken away and I suppose someone else ate them! Our backyard toilet was cleaned out, scrubbed and white-washed. We never entered the realm of poultry keeping again!

The Cold War made Russia the archenemy. During the World War 2 they were our comrades in arms. On our mantelpiece we had a lithograph that consisted of pictures of Churchill, King George and Stalin surrounded by many flags. Uncle Joe was a hero. Later reading of the atrocities that Stalin carried out against his own people came as a shock.

The Jesuits are right. 'Give me a child for the first six years of his life and I will give you the man'.

I have an abiding deeply sympathetic connection to the Russian people!

At school we were very patriotic. There seemed to be constant remembrances and celebrations. The supreme accolade was to be chosen to stand on a chair, holding a large Union Jack on a pole, while everyone exited underneath it. The Assembly Hall had large folding doors, which could be drawn back, but on these occasions everyone exited through the small side door so that all could walk under the flag.

There were many occasions to honour the flag. Empire Day itself. I grew up when most of the world atlas was pink! Armistice Day was observed for many years. I can remember this from Junior School too but I think that by the time I went to Grammar School, the observance had lapsed.

III

'I'll try to see if I know all the things I used to know.'

All small girls of my generation were expected to acquire certain skills. Among these was playing the piano. My mother could play by ear and was sure that her child must also have this power, however deeply hidden. I suppose that I would be 8 or 9 when this torture began. My Aunty Alice, who lived just round the corner, was a music teacher but for some reason I could never fathom I always had to travel further afield.

28

At one dreadful time I had to go to the opposite end of town, immediately after Sunday school. I still have the one and only music certificate presented to me by the London School of Music. It is the very first standard. The amount of practice which achieving this entailed was just incredible.

The piano on which I practiced is in our sitting room. The piano stool still holds some of the music, which I had to learn. I am glad now that I have a basic skill at producing a tune but when facing the rigours of music lessons I could never believe that I would ever admit such a thing.

The agony was further impounded when I changed music teacher. This one resided somewhat nearer to my home but the time of my lesson collided with 'Biggles' on Children's Hour. This was the final straw and even my Mum had to admit that maybe I had reached a musical plateau!

Many years later, as a student, I was part of the College Principal's experimental testing for a 'musical age'. Mine came out at 14, which I thought to be a little on the generous side.

IV

'The bear's ethereal grace.'

Another social attainment was dancing.

Miss Peet's School of Drama and Dance. Miss Peet must

have been made of very stern stuff as the Board advertising her establishment remained up for many years. Is it still there? Do the chubby shadows thump across the floor? Are ghostly taps heard at midnight?

Of course to a small child everyone seems to be enormous and old.

The required dress for dancing class was a maroon tunic with a purple belt. All of us imagined pirouetting around on points but we never reached that heady stage. The ballet shoes were soft slipper type things of the kind that male dancers wear. Tap dancing was more like the real thing as we had proper shoes right from the beginning. On my first exposure to public gaze I remember being copiously sick in the wings but the show had to go on. Along with Noel Coward I can only echo, 'Why'?

Until I reached the stage of being able to rock and roll, my terpsichorean experiences were of the more unfortunate variety.

Queen Mary Tudor said that 'Calais' would be engraved upon her heart. On mine is etched 'The Flowers of Edinburgh'.

In Junior School we had weekly dance lessons. English Country Dancing was all right. It usually involved forming into eights, tripping into the middle and back and then leading off to come back up the middle again, under an arch of arms. This was manageable. I could "Gather Peas-cods" with the best of them.

Scottish Country Dancing was something entirely different.

The basic step is a one-two-three hop. Then all the moves have to be remembered. In groups of four, in to the centre and back to back. Join hands in the middle. Progress!! Any modern child would say, "Get real"!

My partner in crime was Robert Nuttall. I am sure that he too must still bear the bruises. In so much as the Strath Spey and the Eightsome Reel were concerned, he had two left feet. This was at a time when teachers whacked children with their hands or whatever they held in them. Love of the dance for its own self did not figure high on the curriculum. I would desperately volunteer to wind up the record player but I did not often manage to attain this escape route.

Clasping sweaty little hands the Fred and Ginger of Thatto Heath Council School desperately attempted to render complicated dance moves, some of which had to be executed going backwards, while at the same time attempting to avoid physical assault from Mrs. Brown. How this lady managed to land blows I do not know as she had a gammy leg, which was permanently in plaster. Maybe the exercise involved in belting her less lissom students kept her fit.

Every evening a chauffeur-driven Rolls collected her to take her home. She lived just around the corner from us in Crossley Road. She knew all my family and often invited my friends and me to tea.

The fact that even very good little children were beaten was simply an accepted thing. If we had complained our parents would have said that we must have done something to deserve it. I must say we also accepted it as a normal part of life. I cannot remember anyone moaning.

Another male who thwarted my early thespian aspirations was Albert Greenall. This was in Infants School. The Christmas Concert involved "Ornaments on the Christmas tree". Children were different kinds of baubles and I suppose the class goody-goody was the fairy. Albert and I were 'tinsel'. This was no ordinary stringy tinsel. This was pre-war super tinsel. Probably an heirloom piece of tinsel. A long silver gilt chain holding a series of intricate icicle like baubles. We were instructed to handle it very carefully.

We were not called upon to produce a Royal Ballet, standing ovation, multiple bouquet performance, but it did involve carrying the precious garland while declaiming some Yuletide cheer and skipping. Declaiming and carrying were fine, but skipping presented an insuperable problem. Skipping was the one thing that Albert Greenall definitely could not do.
Was there a shortage of boys willing to make a stage appearance? Surely somewhere they could have found a more suitable candidate for fame.
We practiced and practiced. I think I even collared him in the playground in a desperate effort to teach him how to skip.

On the night, I remember skipping gracefully across stage while Albert lolloped along behind, holding high our glittering trophy and attempting not to fall over his still uncoordinated non-skipping feet.

Where is he now? Sitting in a hostelry with a pint of amber liquid, gazing angst ridden deep into its depths, whilst recalling the tinsel debacle and still unable to skip.

V

'Sit down all of you and listen to me.'

At the age of nine I was something of a storyteller and I would even be dispatched to other classes to keep them entertained. My stories involved Bobby Bear and his group. This character came from a Children's Annual but I made up new adventures for them, which centred on St Helens. I was very much into cliff-hanger endings and my friends would badger me to tell them what came next. I had no idea, as I hadn't yet thought of the dénouement.

I inherited this narrative ability from my father. He would tell me the usual fairy stories but instead of going for a walk in the woods, the three bears would go to Mrs. Howard's for fish and chips. Snow White caught the number 7 bus into town and The Three Little Pigs sailed a boat on the lake in Taylor Park, a nearby Park. This lent magic to the mundane. It was a delight to listen and much later I used this device whilst teaching.

At Christmas 1947 my cousin Dorothy gave me a 'difficult' poetry book, *The Grass of Parnassus*. I read it avidly. At school we were expected to learn a poem by heart. From the pages of *Parnassus* I chose "The Ballad of the Inchcape Rock". This ode goes on for about ten pages. It tells the story of the good old Abbot of Aberberthok who placed a bell on the Inchcape Rock. I would drivel on and on…

So little they rose,
So little they fell,
They could not move
The Inchcape Bell

Sir Ralph the Rover was the villain of the piece. He came to a sticky end when his boat was wrecked on the Inchcape Rock, due to his sabotaging of the warning bell.

When I felt that my audience's attention was slipping I would stop, but some days, with a feeling of triumph, I got right through to the end.

Another favourite was "The Destruction of Sennacherib's Host":

'The Assyrian came down like a wolf on the fold'.

I could see him coming:

'And his cohorts were gleaming in purple and gold'.

I had no idea what cohorts were but I was sure that they added greatly to the Assyrian splendour!

'And the sheen of their spears was like stars on the
sea
Where the blue wave rolls nightly on deep Galilee.'

Coming to this fresh and new was marvellous.

'The might of the Gentile, unsmote by the sword
Hath melted like snow in the glance of the Lord'.

The magnificence of the cadencies!

I love the great sonorousness of the Authorized Version of the Bible. In the good old days we read round the class, each taking a verse. I always hoped for a good long chunk that I could read with deep feeling and expression.

Whatever church I attend now a ghastly modern version is used. The passion and the poetry are gone. The magnificent religious and literary heritage is ignored. Show me a church that uses the Authorized Version of the Bible and I will go there.

In the Old Testament the Jews survived. They were the chosen people and God often intervened to save their heroes. In Fairy Tales there were happy endings and good triumphed over evil. I was devastated that God allowed Christ to be crucified. Every Easter I thought that this time God would intervene and save Him.

VI

'We had the best of education.'

In Standard 2, Mrs. Brown's Class, we had singing lessons. Miss Addison played the piano and we trilled our way through such classics as 'The Duke of Plazatoro', whom I suppose inhabits one of Gilbert and Sullivan's operettas and ditties such as 'On Ilkley Moor'.

There was a most unusual lament, supposedly penned

by Bonnie Prince Charlie on his retreat north. "Farewell Manchester, noble town farewell…" I think that few people have bewailed their departure from that city. Imagine poor old Charlie in exotic Italian climes, longing for the North and the days when he was the fair and gallant Prince, instead of a debauched nobody.

My friend Nora was often called upon to do a solo turn:

'Come lasses and lads, get leave of your dads
And away to the maypole gay
Hey ho come to the fair
To the fair in the pride of the morning'

In later years Nora's sister found herself a victim of 'Basher Brown' because she could not equal her sibling's musical talent!

There were two major works of art hanging on the classroom wall. One was the boyhood of Raleigh. The other depicted the legend of Persephone.

Pluto, the God of the underworld, abducted Persephone and took her to Hades. Persephone's mother Demeter tried to find her. Eventually Zeus said that if Persephone had not eaten anything while in Hades, she could then return to Earth. Unfortunately she had eaten some pomegranate seeds. Mrs. Brown's version of the story stipulated that it was six pomegranate seeds. Persephone would still have been able to return if she could have followed the upward path without looking back. Of course she looked back and therefore was only allowed to return to earth for six months of the year. These became the months of spring and summer.

The point at which Persephone looked back was thrilling to portray. We all understood that if Pluto hadn't said "Don't look back", she probably wouldn't have bothered. Telling a child not to do something lends an added temptation to the forbidden activity.

We did not enact Raleigh's boyhood but were inspired by the message the painting held of unknown brilliant futures. Of Raleigh's ignominious demise we knew nothing. We were only aware of his exploits as an Elizabethan hero.

Pandora's Box was another favourite.

Our thespian skills were called upon for many repeats of the 'Baker's Dozen'. A shopper expecting 12 cakes received thirteen. The 'cakes', actually books, were carefully counted out. I have never encountered an actual baker's dozen, but it must have been a tradition at some time.

Discounting our bruises, we received a liberal general education. We were taught that we were the sum of our parts. Ancient Brit, Angles, Jutes and Saxons, Norse and Norman. Tough mongrels.

The story of Augustine who on seeing Anglo-Saxon slaves in Rome said "Not Angles but Angels", applied to me! Blonde and beautiful, I entranced the Roman population! Boadicea, Queen of Iceni, rode her chariot across 2A's classroom.

Balder went out in a blaze of glory after having died at the hand of Loki and the evil mistletoe.

Thor, Wodin and Freya lent their names to the days.

King Arthur regularly burnt the Cakes.

Guy Fawkes crept into the cellars of Parliament.

They all lived and breathed in eager nine-year-olds...

*   *   *

'Reeling and writhing of course to begin with.'

Handwriting was done with pens that had detachable nibs. These pens were dipped into inkwells. Getting a new nib was something of an occasion. The old one had to be produced and declared unusable—only then were we presented with a new one with the admonishment to make it last. Woe betides anyone who appeared to have deliberately crossed his or her nib! We drew pothooks and did writing exercises.

'The Battle of Senlac Hill'—Not many people know that this was the site of the Battle of Hastings, but having had to copy out a brief account of these proceedings many times, as a handwriting exercise, the fact is firmly ingrained in my memory.

Inkwells, which were at the top right-hand corner of every desk, provided an opportunity for the dipping of plaits. My friends Norma, Nora and I sported long plaits and the ends of these were usually a fetching shade of blue having been dipped into the inkwell of the person sitting behind us. I don't remember fulfilling the elevated post of ink monitor but Nora, Brian, Kenneth and I were responsible for a collection of the canvas bags in which each child kept their books and writing materials. These were kept in a corner cupboard.

Chastely and briefly we kissed behind the doors of this cupboard and even more daringly, behind the blackboard. What were we doing there anyway? Brian was my boyfriend and Kenneth was Nora's. Brian brought me oranges. We were together for three years, which come to think of it was longer than any other premarital relationship. On transference to Secondary School we lost touch and on the very rare occasions that we did meet, we studiously ignored each other. Ah, the fickleness of lost love.

Kissing was a real commitment as it meant kissing on the lips. In medieval times the French thought that the English were very promiscuous because they kissed on the lips! The modern day French were considered to have something radically wrong with them as they kissed one another on the cheeks, even the men. Oh, the shame of that! Now everyone kisses the air. Then either one puckered up and made intimate contact or simply avoided the implication that a kiss would be appropriate.

Having survived Mrs. Brown's Class we proceeded to Miss Addison's, truly an outstanding example of 'out of the frying pan into the fire'. Teacher Training establishments of that time must have specified that the main requirements for the education of the young were a strong right arm and a hatred of children.

If we breathed too loudly the recriminations were immediate and painful.

A lifetime later I did some substitute teaching at my old school and found that the class I was due to teach was housed in 'Finnie Addies' room. The pupils had been running riot until they met me. I could not imagine how any child could misbehave with the shade of such a virago hovering in the corner! Fortunately I was able to maintain control without reverting to her Dotheboy methods. I imagine that if I had employed her approach I should have languished long in a cold prison cell.

* * *

'Would it be of any use now?'

The Fishing Ports of England. A large map of the British Isles hung on the classroom wall. Many ports were labelled. Grimsby, Fleetwood, Lowestoft, Whitby. The fishing nets employed by the fishermen of the fishing ports were reproduced in detailed diagrams.

In modern times the purse seine net is most often to be found in *The Times* Crossword; whether or not there are any English fishermen left to use it, is a point to ponder.

Dredgers and Drifters. Dredgers were used to catch flat fish such as sole that frequented the seabed. Drifters caught the more laid back denizens of the ocean that floated lackadaisically, sunning themselves, nearer to the surface.

We sang a song called 'Caller Herring'—'New drawn frae the Forth'. Another rip roaring number, the like of which is not now penned, was

'The Fisher Men of England':

> And a smile upon their lips
> The fishermen of England
> Go down, go down
> To the sea in ships.

The cod, over which trade wars were to be fought, was something that we gave to the cat.

Britannia definitely ruled the waves.

'Cargoes'—Dirty British coaster with the salt-caked smoke stack

> Butting through the Channel in the mad March days.

> 'Oh where are you going to all you big steamers?'
> 'I must go down to the sea again
> To the lonely sea and the sky'.

In our blood stirred the passions of Nelson and Drake.

*   *   *

Learning to sew.

We learnt all kinds of stitches and in the manner of Victorian maidens produced a sample book containing all the stitches that we knew.

Many were the comb cases that we slaved over. The

construction of said case used running and backstitch, whipping and chain stitch. A cornucopia of difficulty and sore fingers.

We made flannelette, winceyette chemises, which we embroidered around the neck and armholes. I cannot even hazard a guess as to when such garments had been in fashion; it was so dreadful that I did not even use mine as a nightdress.

There was also a ghastly shopping bag made from some tough material, which was fiendishly difficult to sew. These could all have been completed in record time if we had been able to use a sewing machine. My mother had a treadle machine and I thought that it was such a waste of time to sew everything as we did in such a labour-intensive way.

Once we made stuffed animals. I made a squirrel. First of course it was necessary to cut the felt into the shapes required. This squirrel held an acorn and had a fiddly gusset underneath so that it could stand up. So many fiddly little bits that could become lost. The disappearance of a small scrap of brown felt had mind numbing repercussions.

I attempted to be 'ill' most Tuesdays to avoid sewing. This strategy became suspect after a while and I had to face up to reality. When the dreaded squirrel was at last completed I presented it to my cousin Michael, who was just a baby. I felt as though I had given him the Crown Jewels, so much blood, sweat and tears had gone into this toy's production.

*   *   *

'She thought it would be quite safe'.

Our way home from Junior School led across the Mushroom Fields. Even then there were no mushrooms to be seen but this was where Silcock's Fair encamped when it came to town. The Fair people lived in caravans. The caravans were not horse drawn, but although modern and motorized they were of a traditional design and exerted a siren-like attraction. I do not know if any of these people were gypsies, but we were warned to stay away from them. Of course the forbidden fruit became even more enticing and we always wandered around the site as the Fair was being set up. We would be invited in to look at the caravans and to me they seemed to be the epitome of what a gypsy caravan should be. Totally filled with exotic clutter.

The expression 'Run away with a black man' had absolutely nothing to do with anyone of African extraction, but referred to gypsies or the Irish. We were told that the gypsies would kidnap us. Well, they didn't!

When the Fair was set up we went back in the evenings. We were again strongly admonished by our parents not to speak to anyone who looked remotely like a gypsy. We went on rides, bought burnt toffee apples and candy floss. Sometimes if we happened to encounter a caravan inhabitant, who was known to us, we would get a free ride or gift. The lights, the music, the sheer exuberance of it all! This exotic establishment decamped after a week. One year would pass before they visited again.

Sometimes gypsies would come to our door selling pegs; flowers made from wood and lucky white heather. They really did say, "Cross my palm with silver". This was quite easy to do in the days of sixpences. It was considered unlucky to turn a gypsy away, so we usually bought pegs. My mother refused to buy the heather as she said she would have to make sure that she never lost it.

*   *   *

'It is wrong from beginning to end'.

Coalfields Glass. The livelihood of my hometown depended on a combination of coal and sand, required ingredients in the making of glass.

A Frenchman introduced the skills of glass blowing. He must have been a Huguenot, as his grave was one of the few preserved in the graveyard that surrounded the Congregational Church in the middle of the town. During the sixties when northern cities were decimated by modern development, this church was demolished. The occupants of any graves were supposedly re-interred. I hope that the Frenchman's malevolent spirit haunts the Bank and Jewellers stores that now cover his resting-place.

I was living in India at this time and could not imagine how this desecration could take place. I returned to find a totally different town centre. Anything of old architectural value had been bulldozed and the dreaded 'Precinct' was all omnipotent. A row of elegant Georgian houses—gone. Inns with ancient foundations—gone. Churches, which marked the rise of nonconformism, the cooperative movement and unionization, all of which advanced the prospects of the workingman—torn down and gone forever.
Two old covered markets—gone.

We had often spent time in the second-hand bookshops and wandered among the many stalls selling items ranging from tripe and cheese to bone china. At Christmas time, kerosene lamps illuminated the stalls, which were bedecked with holly and mistletoe. A scene from Dickens. Probably the stallholders preferred the warmer climes of a precinct, but many portable markets, having medieval roots, simply disappeared forever.

Memory Lane for me is indeed just that, for so many buildings along it now exist only in the mind.

Coal was the lifeblood of local industry. A weed that we called Ginny Green Teeth or Mare's Tails is the direct descendant of the prehistoric fossilized forests, which made up the formation of coal seams. This flora has the individual characteristic of having long fronds, which bear smaller interlocking fronds. It is possible to pull these fronds apart and then try to stick them back together again.

Lying in bed in the evening I could hear the sound of clogs going down the road. Later mining became a fairly well paid job. I cannot imagine anything more awful than to work underground every day. Now that problem does not arise. There are no working pits within the boundaries of the borough.

The town motto 'Ex Terra Lucem' gleams fitfully in the embers of coal fires.

Magnificent sunsets were the direct result of atmospheric pollution. No one ever thought of the quality of the air they breathed. Factories spewed smoke and everyone had coal fires. Although we had all the modern cooking appliances, toast tasted better made over the fire, skewered on a real toasting fork. A kind of metal ring thing hung in the grate and this supported the kettle.

Castles and distant horizons shone in the glowing embers. Fires are very cozy and romantic when a person is not required to make them. We had a coal scuttle full of coal, but at some point in the cold wet weather someone had to trek to the bottom of the backyard where the coal was stored and fill up the scuttle. Then battle the elements to gain the warmth of the house.

The coal boiler heated the water. Of course away from the fire everyone froze. Each bedroom had a fireplace, but unless we were suffering from some fairly dire complaint these were never lit. We had electric fires, but again these were kept against a serious need.

In a later home my mum kept the Victorian hearth and oven while gas fires were installed elsewhere. The Christmas turkey was always cooked there.

In 1958 a friend and I hitch-hiked from Sheffield to St Helens via Manchester. The weather turned very foggy. As we descended from the Snake Pass into the suburbs of Manchester the day turned dark as night. Absolutely as pitch black as the midnight hour. The white fog was now completely black. Street lamps were lit and stores fully illuminated. As we left Manchester and reached the North Lancashire Road the atmosphere cleared. This darkness was terrible industrial pollution.

All men smoked lethal things such as Woodbines and

Capstan, which were of course unfiltered. Women smoking was frowned upon. This is one example of women's social inequality being a blessing.

*   *   *

The Lancashire Cotton Industry.

The received information was that the cotton industry grew up in Lancashire because the area was damp. Could this really be so? Was it damp inside the buildings?

The proximity to the port of Liverpool meant easy transportation of the raw cotton from America. This port served the other transatlantic trade of slaves. England was ambivalent in its support of the Northern forces in the Civil War due to the effect of the supply of cotton to British Industry.

May be time wreaks some kind of vengeance. The Georgian mansions built on trade with the Americas eventually became slums and then fell to the wreckers' bulldozers. The 39 bus that went to Lime Street drove through streets lined with these once elegant abodes. Some were rescued by being incorporated into the University but the majority disappeared.

It is ironic that Gandhi preached against the use of imported cotton cloth in India, when it was the import of cheap cotton goods from India that sounded the death knell of the Lancashire cotton industry.

*   *   *

'Do come back again'.

My Aunty Ethel and Uncle Fred were not blood relatives but long standing friends of my parents. Late in life they performed the ultimate, supreme and incredible crime of moving down south, but this lay far in the future.

Aunty Ethel's mother had left her money. My mother said this money always seemed to have a capital M. They lived in a house in Eccleston and had a car.

Aunty Ethel's father was a total enigma. At this period of time most of the old men I encountered seemed to sit in corners wearing a metaphorical, if not actual, cloth cap doing absolutely nothing. I do not remember Mr. Prescott ever saying anything of his own volition. If my parents inquired after his health he would respond very briefly.

Aunty Ethel and Uncle Fred had one daughter, Iris. One Christmas she made me a great treat—a little house full of presents. One was a Scotty dog brooch and another a green and gold bracelet. I kept these for years after. It was a charming and unusual gift for that time.

My one appearance as a bridesmaid was at Iris's wedding. Her husband Bill was a Catholic so the wedding took place in a Catholic Church. I can still hear my mother warning me not to make an obeisance to anything! I wore a long pink taffeta dress, which made regular stage appearances on others and me, as I was one of the few to own a long dress.

I loved them all dearly. Uncle Fred was the life and soul of the party. That perfect Uncle others wished was theirs. My dad also had a great sense of humour and between the two of them they made my Birthday Parties memorable.

Uncle Fred had one fault—he knew everything. He was right and that was that. He was very fond of conducting to music on the wireless. He had black hair that he would comb sideways, and with the addition of a small painted on moustache, he pranced and preened. A dead ringer for Hitler! We would be convulsed with laughter at his antics.

Songs around the piano were a regular item at any get together. My mum played the piano and she and my Uncle Fred sang duets. These featured old-fashioned numbers such as 'Friend of Mine', 'Only a Rose', 'You are my Heart's Delight' and many others. My Dad's choice was a little more modern. He would warble:

> '...what'll I do when you
> Are far away
> And I am blue
> What'll I do?'

Other favourites were 'The Teddy Bears' Picnic' and 'Run Rabbit'.

Music so potently evokes the past. Hearing 'When you come to the end of a perfect day' or 'The day thou gavest Lord has Ended', I am back at evening service. The setting sun's rays filter through the opaque glass. Not stained glass, as this is a very Low Congregational Church. The desire to place a simple wooden cross on the communion table was the cause of great debate. There is no altar, as an altar indicates that a sacrifice is to be made. Christ had already offered up the supreme sacrifice. The communion table is therefore the centrepiece, where this sacrifice is commemorated in the act of Communion.

They are all there. My dad smelling all clean and dressed up. My mum probably clothed in something that has fur trimmings. The large congregation of colourful characters. They sing: 'As o'er each continent and island, the dawn brings in another day'.

*　　*　　*

Music

Felix Mendelssohn and his Hawaiian Serenaders. Could anything sound less Hawaiian than Felix Mendelssohn? Albert Sandler in the Palm Court of the Grand Hotel. These were popular radio programs. Gigli carolled, but surely Gigli was Italian and therefore an enemy. 'Die ist mein ganze herst' yet again.

My Uncle Fred's car was kept under tarpaulin, as petrol was not available during the war years. My friend Norma and I would peep under the wraps and occasionally sit in it. When it emerged like Sleeping Beauty from a six-year slumber, we all piled in and set off for Southport. The car broke down but we picnicked on the roadside, eventually making our way back, with the sense of achievement felt only by polar explorers.

Beneath my Aunty Ethel's dining room window was a quite extensive rose garden. What kind forbearing people they were! There was never a murmur of complaint as we picked the most beautifully perfumed roses to make scent. The manufacturing process involved mashing the petals in water, then bottling the resulting mush in old medicine bottles. We did not know that it was necessary to extract the essential oil of the flower. How many times we experimented but the result smelled just like water, with maybe the teeniest hint of something floral. The scents of summer roses eluded us but the essence of that experience still lingers.

At the bottom of the garden, just beyond the greenhouse was a small area, which I felt, was my own magic patch. The ground was covered with wild violets, mint and forget-me-nots. One of the slats in the boundary fence could be pulled to one side giving access to the cornfield beyond. Among the corn grew poppies and cornflowers and the occasional field mouse scuttered and climbed. I would sit on the edge of the field and soak up the sun. It would always be like this. Nothing could possibly change.

Years later the violets still grew but beyond the fence was a housing estate.

There was a footpath along the side of one of the fields and in summer we would regularly go for picnics. We walked through the fields until we came to a small store, totally isolated in a sea of corn. Here we bought whatever was available in the way of a snack to help us on our way. Later when sugar was freely available we would buy ice cream. How did this shop survive in such a lonely position? Our cross-country route brought us to the East Lancashire Road. Somewhere along here we climbed a fence to enter a wood.

Picnicking involved a great deal of preparation. When we had our own car the routine did not change much. Great quantities of sandwiches were made the night before, wrapped in greaseproof paper and kept in the coolest possible place. Egg and cress, soggy tomato!

The Primus stove loomed large over the event. We had thermos flasks and it would have been so easy to fill them with tea but it seemed as though it was obligatory to fight the war of the Primus. Usually we won but it was indeed a struggle. First the base of the stove had to be filled with what I think was methylated spirit. It smelled awful and by the time the receptacle was full we had all inhaled enough of the fumes to put us on a raw alcohol high. When the base was ready to be primed a piston was pushed in and out and my brave father lit the issuing gush of meths. This sounds quite a quick process but the pumping was not always immediately successful. Often the whole rig would fall over. It all seems very dangerous and I am sure that such lethal monstrosities are now banned.

The resulting tea had that *je ne sais* flavour usually enjoyed by the denizens of Skid Row. We drank from the pout of Bakelite cups, further enhancing the charm of the exotic brew.

Whatever the season the ants were ready. Earwigs ran them a close second. When bluebells were in season we collected huge sheaves of flowers along with several earwigs.

If I needed to 'go', it had to be in the undergrowth, inevitably among the bramble bushes. There was a pretty pool, the delightful haunt of midges. It was with a collective sigh of relief when we returned to the comfort of home—bitten but unbowed and already planning the next outing.

*   *   *

'Her hair grows in such long ringlets.'

My hair is straight, absolutely straight, not a hint of a curl anywhere. I am sure that the influence of Shirley Temple's curly mop inspired mothers of that time to picture their little darlings in the same tonsorial style. Plaits were bad enough. The combing of such long hair was painful. An added torture was to have sections of hair wrapped in rags. These had to stay in place all night and caused incredible discomfort. The ensuing ringlets were tied up in bunches.

This was of course very many years before the emergence of Rastafarians. Unknowingly many English seven-year-old girls led an avant-garde movement in ethnic hairstyles, albeit only during the witching hours. Curling tongues of medieval design were heated in the fire. The use of these presented the danger of branding on the forehead. The smell of burning hair was a normal precursor to Sunday school.

Later I spent many unhappy sessions at the hairdressers, suffering perms and styling. Eventually I asserted myself and had my hair cut short, only growing it again when ponytails came into fashion.

*   *   *

'That's very curious.'

The liberty bodice. This was in vogue into the early fifties. It was an undergarment for girls. A short fleecy lined vest, which went over the actual vest. The bodice had narrow satin strips down the front. The shedding of this apparel was like a Victorian maiden putting up her hair. It was a signal of burgeoning puberty. The bra lurked around the corner once the liberty bodice had gone. What happened to all the liberty bodice makers?

What happened to the gentlemen's hat makers? Cloth caps, trilbies, bowlers, where are they now? The racing fraternity and certain City Bankers appear to patronize the mad hatters, but in general men no longer wear hats as a social must.

The ladies corset makers, where are they?

My mum had a problem with her back and so had to wear corsets as a support but at one time most ladies wore them. They resembled part of a suit of armour with an awesome profusion of suspenders dangling from them. The rigid supports, which controlled the female figure, were made of Whalebone.

Was it for such as this that Captain Ahab gave his life and Great White Whale Moby Dick drew the *Pequod* and nearly all its crew to the bottom of the sea?

Prior to the introduction of nylon, women wore silk or lisle stockings. The ladies had to perform contortionist-like gyrations in order to fasten these to their back suspenders.

Thank goodness I was too young to experience these anthropological phenomena. I observed in the manner of a foreign explorer fascinated by tribal dress.

Gloves.   Cold weather gloves are still around and the Queen wears elbow length numbers but the tradition of glove wearing has gone. I was a teenager in the fifties.   I could not have imagined going out formally unless I wore stockings and gloves. My mum and I shared a vast collection of gloves. They were so pretty. This was a totally sexist regime. To look pretty was desirable. A particularly elegant pair of gloves was of grey cotton with small seed pearl embellishments.   When I wore them I felt like something out of *Little Women*. White nylon with white dots. White on white, very fashionable. My Mum had an elbow-length pair in blue. Gloves, shoes and hats had to match.

School Uniform.

This still exists and I think is a very egalitarian mode of dress but children's attitude towards the style of it must have changed.

I passed the scholarship exam. and proceeding to Grammar School meant the purchase of a uniform. There was also a very long list of other necessities.

The uniform was bottle green. A bottle-green tunic, lighter green blouse, a green and blue striped tie and bottle-green knickers. These were Aunty Annie type bloomers with elastic round the knee! Outdoor wear included a green mackintosh, a green hat with blue and green band and sensible flat shoes with short white socks.

When my friends and I were geared up in our new regalia, we looked rather like Droopy of Seven Dwarves fame. All our clothes were bought to last, so they trailed along behind us. I do not know how much taller our mothers expected us to grow. Maybe everything shrank? We were not at all embarrassed by our appearance as all the green horns were similarly caparisoned. I cannot imagine that the Gap-clad and Reebok-booted teenagers of today would accept such a fate with equanimity.

Name tapes had to be sewn on each garment. These were Cash's name tapes and I am glad to say I recently bought some of their woven products.
God Bless the Weavers of Coventry!

In summer we wore green and white check dresses—an unflatteringly gathered skirt and bodice top that did nothing for the developing bosom. My mother was something of a dressmaker and when flared skirts came into fashion she made my school dresses in a somewhat more fashionable style. The non-conformist streak!

My hat, which was made of bottle-green velour, was held in place by a piece of elastic under the chin. The fashion was to steam the chapeau so that the sides turned up in cowboy fashion. Many odd little touches became *de riguer*. At one point no one who was 'in' would fasten her mackintosh belt around the waist; this had to be doubled back on itself and fastened at the back. The sash, which went round the tunic, must always hang at the side; never at the back.

The first clothes memory that I have entails a buttonhook. This is truly in the realms of the Victorian. I wore leggings, which fitted snugly, to keep me warm once these had been put on over my dress. The lower part of the leg parts needed to be tightly fastened. There was no stretch fabric in those days. Several very small buttons and buttonholes were on each side of the leg and a strap went under the foot. All these had to be fastened with a buttonhook, as they were too fiddly for the fingers. Extrication was performed in the same manner.

I remember a red coat with fur trim. The fur moulted all over me. I accelerated the process by plucking away at the itchy stuff.

Poke bonnets. To buy a pig in a poke means to buy a pig in a bonnet. An unwise choice. These chapeaux were usually of white straw with pink and white rosebuds. I have seen photographs of modern-day Japanese infants wearing millinery such as this.

Pixie hoods. The pixie hood tied under the chin and looked vaguely Scandinavian. Did the Vikings reach Lancashire? An easy sewing project to keep idle hands busy was the making and embroidering of a pixie hood.

The utility mark. This was a symbol on clothes made during the war. It resembled inverted commas facing backwards. I expect that such marked garments would be collectors' items now!

Everything was prone to shrinkage.

Girls did not wear trousers and tights had not been invented. This meant that in cold weather the young female froze. We were toughened up ploughing through the snow.

Boys wore Just William type short trousers. Their changing to the wearing of long trousers was a rite of passage similar to the female abandonment of the liberty bodice.

In the 50s wearing trousers was very avant-garde. During the war women wore trousers, but somehow this very practical fashion had disappeared. I read somewhere that the wearing of men's clothes was in earlier times held to be one of the proofs of witchcraft. Maybe some forgotten fear lurked deep in the psyche.

When I was in college a female wearing trousers would occasion wolf whistles. At that time a male was not instantly towed away to be hung, drawn and quartered if he wished to express his baser emotions in this way.

Not yet having discovered that sitting in the bath while wearing cotton trousers made them skin tight, the only recourse was to take in the seams. Blue jeans were not commonly popular. We always attended lectures in dresses or skirts and wearing stockings. At one period I wore brightly coloured knee socks. As skirts were long these gave the appearance of stockings. Quite daring apparel.

The great role model for older teenagers (did we call ourselves that?) was Bridget Bardot. Her tweety French accent was very off putting but that did not deter the desire to follow her fashion lead. The first necessary asset was a ponytail. This was absolutely essential. Sleeveless, moderately low cut blouses, nipped in waists and full skirts were the thing. At least Miss Bardot had a natural shape. None of us desired to have the flat as a board, modern model figure. In order to achieve the full-skirted look we bought stiff net petticoats. After washing these were soaked in diluted sugar! Were we totally mad? Did wasps and bees not assail us whenever we sallied forth? Fortunately this was a brief necessity as hooped boned underskirts were invented.

We wore girdles. These were a definite improvement on Captain Ahab's corsets but they were still restrictive. My mother offered the dire warning that if I ever stopped wearing a 'support' my muscles would totally turn to jelly and I would spread in all directions like a recalcitrant blancmange. How right she was!

The Empire Line was a fashion suited to all. The high bodice *a la* Jane Austen heroines and Napoleon's Josephine was flattering to all. My mother turned up trumps again and made me several dresses of this design. A lovely soft blue wool was the most attractive. Unfortunately this style was not popular for very long and I spent much time altering everything to achieve a figure-hugging effect. Dressing correctly was very important.

At College the principle of sharing was paramount. Six of us exchanged wardrobes. As we were of very disparate sizes and colouring this was something of a challenge. I had a stole, white with gold thread. By the time I got a chance to wear it, it was rather limp, as it had gone the rounds of all my friends, even spending a weekend in Castleton. I stretched dresses belonging to others, as my bosom was always prominent. Bright electric blue was popular. I wore my friend Wendy's coat with great regularity. Once I dieted for a week to fit in a pink chiffon number. The dress I wore when I first met my husband lies folded in my closet.

*   *   *

'Take your choice'.

Legends are very attractive and there is a duty to pass them on.

My contribution is that my forefathers fought with Cromwell. Cromwell is my all-time favourite historical character, closely followed by Henry V.

My father's family came from Warrington, which I think is the only town outside of London to have erected a statue of The Protector. Gleave is not a very common name and in the 1700's a Johannes Gleave lived in Warrington. I imagine that the family descended from him. Some Americans have this burning desire to trace their roots. I think most English people know that their families have been around from the year dot and so don't bother. As Lord Hume succinctly pointed out, "Even Mr. Wilson must be the fourteenth Mr. Wilson."

At the time of the Civil War South West Lancashire was mainly pro-Royalist, The Earl of Derby being a local example.

Warrington's support of the Roundhead cause was exceptional and I just know that the Gleaves were there. I doubt that they were commissioned and I recently read that rosters of that time did not record the names of foot soldiers. This legend can then remain intact, as it can neither be proved nor disproved. The mists of Avalon cannot be penetrated nor the Towers of Camelot stormed to reveal a square table.

After the war my mother decided to open a dress and general haberdashery shop. Coupons were still needed for the purchase of clothes and other materials. It was possible for an incipient small business to receive Government encouragement in the form of an extra coupon allowance. My mother was denied this incentment. Harold Wilson was then the Head of the Board of Trade. Mum made an appointment to see him and argue her case. His reply to her was that as my father had not been on front-line service during the war, the extra coupon allowance could not be made.

My mother replied, "During the war everyone was considered to be in the front lines!" She opened her store and ran it successfully for many years.

Did she really beard the lion in his den? It's a legend.

My dad, who was not considered to have been on the front line, was a Special Constable and Fire Warden after having worked a twelve-hour shift in a factory. One evening at the height of the blackout, a friend and he were on patrol. They went into a shelter for a smoke and were contentedly puffing away when they realized that there was no roof. Apparently the Luftwaffe could have spotted their glowing cigarettes from the far distance of Berlin.

Galahad and Bedivere could have caused havoc with their fire ritual.

Whenever there was a shoot my great-grandfather, who worked on Lord Derby's estate, would be employed as a beater. King Edward VII was a regular visitor. On one occasion my great-grandfather was helping to propel the innocent grouse and pheasant to their doom, when a shot went awry and pierced his 'Billy Cock' hat. The King was very apologetic and the hat became a treasured possession.

Did Edward really speak to my great-grandfather? How many hats carry a similar story?

The great and noble king had recognized one of the peasants.

My Uncle Norman was killed in Flanders in the First World War. As I felt that someone remaining should visit his grave, I wrote to the War Office. I received a prompt reply to the effect that he has no known grave. His name is on the Menin Gate in Ypres. He belonged to the Liverpool Scottish Regiment and on a visit to Edinburgh Castle I saw his name in the Book of Remembrance. It is also on the Cenotaph in town. It is a name. The person lives in our remembering. A large photograph of him in his kilted uniform hangs in my home. The citation that the family received is beneath it. His medals are in a box, which were issued to all the soldiers. The box is decorated with a bas-relief of the Princess Royal. Inside is a letter written to him by my mother, bearing the impression of the forget-me-nots, which the letter states she enclosed. How did it get back to her?

This was the lost generation. I never saw him but he is very real to me.

His fiancée Alice Boyson never looked at anyone else after his death. She was a music teacher and though not really my Aunt, was known in the family circle as Aunty Alice and was invited to all-important family occasions. She was the organist at my wedding.

This dramatic lost love appealed to my romantic nature.

> 'The flowers left thick at nightfall in the wood
> This Eastertide calls into mind the men
> Now far from home, who, with their Sweethearts, should
> Have gathered them and will do never again'.

> 'The pallor of girls' brows shall be their pall,
> Their flowers the tenderness of patient minds,
> And each slow dusk a drawing-down of blinds'.

Alice was one of those girls, who drew down the blinds on their own youth and on that of their shadow children waiting in the firelight. 'Loved and were loved.'

Did she truly never wish to marry, or were there simply not enough men left for her to make a choice? This is a legend and Alice 'was born into this solitude'.

> 'The Cherry Trees bend over and are shedding
> On the old road where all that passed are dead,
> Their petals strewing grass as for a wedding
> This early May morn when there is none to wed.'

Beside my Uncle's picture is a table upon which are some of the books that Alice received as Sunday School Prizes: *Frank Horton's Heritage* "presented to Alice Boyson. St John's Sunday School. Ravenhead 1900."
The Gates of Eden "Awarded to Alice Boyson. Miss Itall's Class. Reverend G. J. Bolton. Supt. John Anders. 1906-1907". There is a quote from Tennyson on the first page of this book:

'Saw distant gates of Eden gleam
And did not dream it was a dream.'

*   *   *

'What sort of people live about here?'

Every family has its black sheep and at least according to my mother the one in my father's family was Uncle Sid. He could not always have been considered to be so because he was best man at my parents' wedding. His progress on the path to perdition was accelerated by his marriage to my Aunt Maggie. The fact that she was referred to as Aunt, rather than Aunty, set the tone for the relationship.

Why would anyone wish the graceful name of Margaret to be changed to Maggie?

My mother's attitude to Maggie was exactly that of the Queen Mother to Mrs. Simpson. I know Maggie did not blow in from Baltimore but the phrase 'that woman' hovered menacingly in the air whenever her name was mentioned. In appearance Maggie somewhat resembled the Duchess of Windsor. She was tall and skinny and her dark hair was closely coiled creating a hint of the Medusa. At any moment her tresses could have unravelled and menacingly attacked us all.

The Crown Prince's future had been devastated by an unfortunate liaison.

My father had lent Sid some money when he could ill afford to do so. Dad always treated Sid and Maggie in his usual warm and pleasant manner but something had deeply upset my mother. The reasons lie buried in the past.

Maggie was also a 'cinder sitter'. I can hear the warning inherent in those words echoing through time. 'Cinder sitter' ranked high on my Mum's list of the undesirable, at the top of which was 'common'. The advent of central heating has caused cinder sitters to disappear. Sitting too near the fire caused a horrible mottled effect to appear on the shins. The implication was also that anyone who could spend so much time sitting in front of a fire must be bone-idle.

Uncle Sid was lost to us. As adamantly as Queen Mary would not receive Wallis, so my mother dissociated herself from any gathering where Maggie might be present. If they were already at my Aunty Annie's house when we visited, a certain frisson filled the air and an excuse would be made to leave as soon as possible.

Aunty Annie was my father's eldest sister. There were seven siblings. Annie, Nellie (Helen), Tom, Sydney, Alfred, William and my father Ernest. Enid, Aunty Annie's daughter, later found that family records revealed that there had been two older children, Albert and Victoria.

My Grandma and Grandpa Gleave were not as close to me as my maternal Grandmother. They brought to mind the tiny figures that go in and out of those little houses that predict the weather. When my Mum and Dad married, my Granny Gleave did not speak to them for over a year. My

Mum said that it was because my father's pay packet went to support his new household and not that of his parents.

My Grandfather had a waxed moustache and when he kissed me it prickled my face. I am told that my Granny had a great sense of humour but I do not recall that.

The family was poor compared to that of my mother. They had furniture, which now would be treasured antiques. In particular I recall a very elegant chaise longue, which was unceremoniously pushed under the stairs. The back of my legs stuck to the leather whenever I sat on it. I have a small console table that belonged to them. Of course furniture was carefully handed down when family members could not afford anything new.

The advent of hire purchase in the 50s meant that it was possible for most people to acquire new things. A great deal of long preserved 'old stuff' was summarily discarded.

My Aunty Annie lived across the road from her parents. My Uncle Ernie had been a glass blower, which was a skilled and well-paid profession, but the pressure on the lungs could cause disease. I do not know what it was called but he had developed this affliction. He could not have been all that old when I was small but he was another one of those old men who sat in a corner saying and doing nothing. This was before the advent of television, when we can now all sit happily doing nothing. I could not imagine that he had ever been young and in love.

What happened to these men? Had life been so tough that they had simply opted out? The women were cheerful and resilient but the males seemed to have crumbled.

I found their house a fascinating but undesirable residence. Much later I found that it was rented, another sin in my mother's book. Anyone with a grain of sense moved heaven and earth to buy their own home. The house consisted of three downstairs rooms. I never went upstairs. Presumably there were three bedrooms as my cousins Enid and Dorothy lived there too. They had no bathroom. There was no hot water. The sink in the kitchen was made of a rough stone that could scratch the hands. This was called a slop stone. I am sure that later some kind of water heater was installed. The lavatory in the backyard was another gem of history. There was never any toilet paper but newspaper cut into squares.

I once went, with my friend Norma to stay with her Grandmother in Maghull. Norma was my best friend from about the age of eight or nine though we were friends from the age of three or four. We were both only children, so we were the siblings we never had. An earlier friend called Margaret had left with her family to go to London. Her father had been a violinist at the local theatre. In later years it puzzled me as to how he supported quite a large family on this income.

In or I should say outside of Norma's granny's house was the most inconvenient plumbing I had then encountered. The only means of sanitation was an outhouse at the end of the garden. This did not have a cesspool and had to be regularly cleaned out by some department of the local Council. I contemplated with horror the possibility of having to get up during the night and trek through the wilderness.

The middle room of Aunty Annie's house was the pantry and what should have been the dining room. It took me some time to puzzle out why this room was not used, when space was at a premium. Then I realized that there was no way of heating this room and so it was virtually ignored.

A huge table took up most of the space in the front living room. There was a large ornately carved sideboard and a sofa. My Uncle Ernie was permanently ensconced in a small chair in the corner near the fire.

The sideboard was full of old objects including an ancient clock and two bronzes, one of Perseus holding the Gorgon's head and some other Greek hero. On one wall was a morbid still life of some dead birds. On another hung an ancient barometer.

There was so little room for visitors that my cousin Derek and I would always sit under the table. This was covered by a heavily fringed maroon tablecloth, which hung down, practically to the floor. Once we were under there our imaginations took flight. Bedouin camps, Polar expeditions, Indian tepees. The firelight glowed through the cloth, adding another element of enchantment.

We ate our jam sandwiches, having argued as to who should have the crust, and transported ourselves far from Borough Road.

My Aunt lived in this house for over seventy years. The door was never locked.

Another place, which would now be an antique dealer's dream, was the room behind Aunty Evelyn's bakery shop.

All the old rubbish was in here. The back rooms of these houses had no space under the floor. The houses were built on a slope. The front room, which was the bakery shop, had a wooden floor and a space underneath but the floor of the back room was tiled on a base under which was simply soil. These were the places where Victorian murderers could bury their victims, often under the hearthstone.

One such as these had lived in Rainhill. A military gentleman and a pillar of the community announced that his wife and child had gone to visit relatives in Australia. Those were the days when such an undertaking was expensive, unusual and very time consuming. The only communication was by sea mail, so that many months could pass before any correspondence would be received. No one considered it unusual that nothing was heard from the travellers. Eventually such a long period of time passed that the lady's relatives became suspicious. A detailed search of the premises resulted in the discovery of the remains of mother and child, buried under the kitchen floor.

The tiles in Aunty Evelyn's backroom were black and red. A round table with hairy paw feet took pride of place. The mantle was a repository for old clocks and ornaments. Several different designs of old dining and armchairs stood around. There was also the ubiquitous chaise longue. Around the front of the fireplace was a brass fender, which ended in two small upholstered seats. There were the requisite fire irons. Anything in that room would now be considered a collector's item. I looked at albums full of intricately designed and beautifully embroidered old Valentine and Birthday Cards.

*　*　*

Evelyn

Aunty Evelyn was the eldest of my mother's half-sisters. As far back as I could remember she had grey hair, but she would regularly draw me to one side saying that she did not have a single grey hair in her head. This she attributed to the fact that she rinsed her hair with vinegar, thus in her mind at least, preserving the auburn tresses of her youth. She also laboured under the delusion that she did not have a single line on her face, probably due to witch hazel or some such herbal potion. This too I'm afraid was far from the truth, but no one ever disagreed with her. She was married to Uncle Walter, a very patient long-suffering individual.

In those days marriage meant marrying the whole family.

In present times families are seldom so large and members may eventually live in different continents. Back then relatives played major roles on life's stage.

By profession Aunty Evelyn was a confectioner and my Aunty Gertie and on her retirement, my Aunty Sue, worked in her business and lived over the shop. Apart, they were the most pleasant people but when together, the sparks flew! (I am sure that my parents must have argued, but I never heard or saw them do so). On our visits to Cambridge Road where they lived, I watched open mouthed, fascinated by the passionate outbursts. The interludes of operatic intensity were usually caused by the inability of one or the other of

71

them to locate previously ordered bread! Accusations flew across the room like tracer bullets. The air crackled with impassioned assertions and denials. The pandemonium only came to an end when there was a general need to draw deep breaths. The problem was usually resolved and my Aunty Evelyn maintained that though they argued they never sulked!

Whenever she sent me a Birthday Card or letter she would write 'mazeltov' on it. I do not think that we had any Jewish connections and wonder where she acquired this exotic exultation.

*   *   *

Anne Zillah

Aunty Sue whose real name was Anne Zillah, was second in line. My mother said that she had never married because in order to find a man who could live up to her expectations, she would have to 'draw one'. Meaning that her levels of perfection could not possibly exist in any flesh and blood creature.

I was deeply fascinated by the fact that when she talked, her false teeth chattered away quite independently. I wished that I had such fascinating dentures. What with my Aunty Sue's teeth and the dramatic 'bread' scenarios, visits to Cambridge Road were never without excitement. When I was really small she would sing me the following ditty:

> Paddy Magee forgot that he was dead.
> He sat up in his coffin and he said,

'In another forty minutes, Topsy will be in it.'
When Paddy Magee forgot that he was dead.

A charming cradle song.

My Aunty Sue was renowned for hoarding clothes and throwing out everything else. She had drawers full of exquisite, though ancient lingerie. She bought dresses, coats and hats that she never wore. There were drawers full of delicate lace handkerchiefs and detachable lace collars and cuffs, which had long gone out of fashion.

She was the last of my mum's half-sisters to survive and was reputed to have discarded many valuable items.

*   *   *

Gertrude

Aunty Gert was elegant and gentle and would have made a perfect wife and mother. So many men were killed in the First World War that there was a shortage of potential grooms. She remained single. She had affection for one of the salesmen who visited the shop. My mother possibly toned down, or spiced up her version of what ensued.

Aunty Gert's romance was cut short when her beau returned to Ireland. As the gentleman concerned was an Irish Catholic, this was truly a walk on the wild side. He wrote to her and she wrote back, but her letters were returned.

I often wondered why Gert had not gone to Ireland to find out. She visited the Isle of Man and Ireland was only a little further. Passion died and my Aunty Gert filled her life with work and church.

A small glimpse into the 'Catholic' situation. Many years later a cousin married a Catholic. None of the aunts went to the wedding and my Aunty Evelyn refused to present her usual wedding gift, which was a canteen of cutlery.

*   *   *

Vagaries

My mother, who was not emotionally enthralled by *object d'art*, lamented the fact that my Grandmother had given a painting of Good King Billy to Dr Bates, a neighbour. Why Dr Bates should have been given our painting I could not understand. He lived in some splendour in a large house adjacent to the park.

I once visited this edifice and found it to be dank, dark and dismal. There was a pervading, heady mixture of metal polish and mouse. Ghastly things like elephant feet umbrella stands lurked in corners. Portraits of miserable Victorians adorned the walls. Tiger rugs with green glass eyes glowered up. Of Good King Billy I saw no sign.

Our family doctor was Dr Kyle. He was an Orange man. Why I was informed of this I do not know. He didn't look very orange, although the general opinion was that he enjoyed a drop of the hard stuff and his nose had a purplish tinge. Maybe he ate oranges, or had eaten a surfeit of them in the past? I stored this information away as just another adult oddity, waiting for him to reveal any element of the mysterious orangeness. Much later I realized that he belonged to the Orange Order, whose allegiance to William of Orange is still total.

On holiday we visited the spot in Devon where good old Billy had come ashore. The interwoven history of radical Protestantism. I am sure that my mother had little knowledge of William of Orange but he was enshrined as one of the good guys.

There were several superstitions that could only have had their history in Paganism. They certainly did not fit into the non-conformist clean in which everything had to be thought out and an individual opinion reached.

Hawthorn trees produce beautiful pink, white and red blossoms, but the branches are also covered in thorns. We had several of these trees in the back garden of our last house. My natural reaction was to bring flowering bows into the house. This was totally and absolutely forbidden. Apart from the fact that the thorns were very sharp I could see no good reason why this plant should be so ostracized.

Apparently, in pre-Christian times, a cutting from the hawthorn tree was presented to the person who was to be sacrificed to expiate the gods. The story goes that a follower gave the ill-fated Charles I a sprig of hawthorn, on the eve of his last battle. Christ also wore a crown of thorns.

Another banned item was lilac. I have found no explanation

for this. Red and white flowers together are inauspicious.

Of course the better-known superstitions prevailed. Crossed knives indicated a quarrel. 'Stir with a knife, stir for strife.' No walking under ladders. Never open an umbrella in the house. If I spill salt I always throw a pinch over my left shoulder, with my right hand, for there sits the devil.

In India and America black cats are considered to be unlucky. In England a black cat crossing one's path is a sign of good luck. This excludes a neighbour's cat, which loves to sleep in my front garden, later using it as a toilet. Maybe it *is* lucky in that it has not yet been drenched with water!

The cat was considered to be a witch's familiar animal, so whether meeting a cat would result in good or bad fortune, might depend on one's relationship with the witch.

*   *   *

'All in the golden afternoon.'

When the beaches were cleared of barbed wire and whatever other anti-enemy devices, we made a yearly pilgrimage to Blackpool. We left from Thatto Heath Station. I recall the thrill as the train approached. Standing there clutching my bucket and spade, the anticipation of a week beside the sea was almost too much.

Our 'digs' were always at the North Shore, as my mum felt that this was the classy area. We walked from the station to the boarding house. At the end of the road was a tantalizing glimpse of the water. After settling in, it would be time for tea. This was high tea. Cold meats and salad. Cakes, scones, cups of very strong tea. All I could think of was the beach.

Refreshed and strengthened, we would change our clothes and head seawards. Usually at this time the tide was so high that it was not possible to go on to the sands. We would stroll along the prom. Eventually the sea air having made us peckish we bought fish and chips. Meals provided at our digs were breakfast, lunch, tea and supper.

Usually my Uncle Billy, Aunty Nellie and Derek would meet up with us there. My father, who never touched porridge at home, considered it a holiday must. Breakfast, in those blissfully cholesterol-free days, always consisted of fried bacon and eggs, tomatoes and mushrooms and a real killer, fried bread.

After breakfast, while my Mum and I prepared for the day ahead, my father would stroll down to the seafront for a copy of the *Daily Express*.
If it should be raining he would report that there was a little sea mist in the air! This optimistic assessment of a cloudy day made us all the more determined to be out there, seeking the elusive sun.

One place of utter enchantment, which I am sure has long since disappeared, was Fairyland. This was not a part of the Fair, but a separate building. Entering from the street one was instantly transported into another world. Gondolas sailed through mystical tableau of flower-garlanded glades. Fairy-like mannequins swayed and twirled while music filled the air. The gondolas made two full circumnavigations, so that the passengers could enjoy the tableau on both sides.

I could have stayed in this magical place all day long.

Blackpool Tower was another must. There was a zoo in the basement. I now realize this was a dreadful place to keep animals. There was also a circus. As a finale the ring was flooded. How did they do that?

We always visited the Fair but after I had outgrown the roundabouts, I found that the number of rides that I could stomach was very limited. I have never been able to go on any of the sick-making rides such as the Big Dipper. The majority of the contraptions were guaranteed to scare or sicken.

My favourite ride was the cocks. Why was it called the cocks when it was a carousel made up of horses? These went around and up and down in a sedate manner. Bumper cars were fine as they did not swoop down a gradient but simply crashed into one another.

All these were great, but the greatest of all was the Beach. The very first thing I would always do was to go for a ride on a donkey. Derek and I built castles, bathed in the sea, collected shells and seaweed. We would watch the sea come in and fill the moat of the castle we had built. There were small flags, which we planted on the turrets.

Even a Lancashire Summer would sometimes produce strong sunshine and I would experience that once-in-a-year feeling of cool smooth sheets against my sunburned skin. Some people lived here all year round. How I envied them.

Holidays were the time we took photographs. Just about the only time when we took photographs. Our camera extended like a concertina and focusing took a very long time. Extracting and inserting a film was a major exercise. It could not have required total darkness, as no one would have been able to see anything, but it seemed to require darkness and seclusion.

I have a sentimental corner for Blackpool. It may be vulgar but it has no pretensions, with its smell of doughnuts, fresh shrimps and candyfloss.

The Blackpool Illuminations came along later. It took some time for resorts to gear up after the war.

When it became safe to sail across the Irish Sea we took our holidays in the Isle of Man. Mines had been laid in the ocean and these had to be removed before commercial shipping could resume. This was a time when Liverpool still had a thriving dockland. We always packed as if the places we were to visit had no facilities whatsoever. All kinds of toilet goods were taken.

Even though it was for just a week, the English weather demanded the full gamut of clothes. I longed to experience the height of sophistication and go away for two weeks.

This was a time when credit cards did not exist and checks were seldom used. All our holiday money was in cash. My Dad had a special pocket sewn into his vest. In this pocket reposed our vacation money. I usually received extra spending money from my aunts.

The boat crossings must have been smooth, as I do not recall any of them. There was a great thrill in seeing land again. I think that on every occasion we visited the Isle of Man, Aunty Ethel, Uncle Fred and Iris came with us. We stayed in Douglas. We caught the little train that took us to the various glens. I have never been back in recent years, so I do not know how commercialized the area has become. At the time when we went, we were often the only people to alight from the train. Wild pinks grew among the heather. Gorse and vetch covered the hillsides. Great bushes of un-pruned roses filled the air with perfume. Whenever I see vetch, even on an abandoned site, it brings back those long-ago days.

My parents had visited before the War and remembered when these places had buzzed with people. I loved them the way they were.

We would climb Laxey Wheel. Wandered through the Rose Gardens of Castle Rushen. Explored Peel Castle and on our tour of the TT Race circuit, bade 'Good Day' to the 'little people' as we crossed the fairy bridge.

We found a little cove that we claimed as ours. The water was a brilliant Mediterranean blue. It was quite safe to swim there and this is where we spent most mornings swimming in our own private haven.

Much as I should like to revisit I do not think that I ever will.

When we travelled to Blackpool by car, several miles from St Helens the road curved and there was a hump-backed bridge. Immediately on the right was a Georgian house. Every time we passed this house I secretly vowed that when I was grown up I should live there.

Years later on being driven to Blackpool I hoped to see the house again. Of course there are now motorways taking cars cross-country directly to Blackpool and I have no idea how I could find my lost dream. Its foundations may even lie beneath the all-consuming tarmac. The same may be true of past summer afternoons spent in the Manx glens. I do not intend to find out.

*   *   *

A present intrusion.

Since I began writing several changes have occurred. We moved from our house in Chicago to a house in Florida. We also purchased a house in Sutton Coldfield, near Birmingham, in order to be near our daughter and her family who live in Coventry. Our son and his wife live in Connecticut.

The idea is to spend summer in England and the colder months in Florida.

Present situations soon become past experiences to record. When I speak to people who have spent all their lives in one place, I can only gaze in amazement.

It is fortunate that we both suffer from itchy feet. My husband, who is a workaholic, recently had the possibility of taking up a job in Wyoming, a very cold U.S. State. It wasn't something that he seriously considered but the offer was there. I must admit that just for a second my eyes lit up at the prospect of new horizons!

* * *

Grammar School

I passed the Scholarship exam. and with my friends Norma and Nora proceeded to Cowley Girls Grammar School. This institution had been founded by Sarah Cowley (a Congregationalist), 'for the educations of poore peoples children'. Those who did not pass the exam. went to secondary schools. I totally lost contact with any of our friends who did not make it. This was also an all girls' school, so boys disappeared from the regular scene too.

* * *

Magic

I am sure that my children will expect their births to be top of the list.
These were magnificent experiences resulting in total joy, but I think that any mother, even one like me who had a relatively easy time, will consider that the amount of pain and stress involved relegate giving birth from the 'magic' category.

The moment when one holds a new-born child is pure magic. The effort involved in reaching that situation isn't!

Chapter 2

Memoirs of Friends & Families
of Audrey Carole Sanyal

Introduction

Above is her account of her childhood in her own words.

Continuation of her autobiography was interrupted by her research into genealogy followed by the two books that she wrote and then her sudden death put a stop to going on any further.

Our children and I decided to follow it up with her biography and invited her friends and my relatives for their impressions.

We were very pleased with the response.

Her school friend Norma, her Sheffield University friends Wendy and Mary, Jenny one of her fellow teachers when she taught in London, Santimoy my brother and his wife

Anurupa from India, nephew Tarun from LA, our son Neil, Shomita his wife and Shanta our daughter agreed to share their memories.

Our son-in-law felt that his thoughts of Audrey are his own and didn't want to share.

I made an attempt to record our life together.

Chapter 2.1

Memories of Norma Smyth, Audrey's earliest friend

THE EARLY YEARS

In 1942 Audrey was four years old. The world was at war and small children went to school early. In her case the school was Ravenhead St John's Infant school in St Helens.

St Helens is a town that owes its development to the Industrial Revolution. In the first half of the twentieth century you would have looked out of your window to see a view punctuated by pit heads and tall chimneys spouting polluting smoke that blackened all the buildings. Huge slagheaps rose with the waste from the mines and the canals reputedly contained exotic fish in the warm effluent from the factories.

St Helens was most famous for Pilkington Glass; one of its factories, Ravenhead, stood near the school. Audrey's father worked at United Glass Bottle Manufacturers. Glass dominated the town. It is a measure of how much England has changed that if you Google 'Ravenhead' now, it turns out to be a retail centre.

It was in the playground of Ravenhead School that Audrey and I met. Even at that age, she was as warm and friendly as she remained all her life. In due course the kindly regime of Miss Billington, the Infant school Head, was replaced by the altogether tougher Head of Thatto Heath Primary School. It still exists.

In those days young children were allowed to walk to school with their friends. Audrey and I lived quite close to each other in a district usually called Toll Bar, so we would meet and make our way to Bates Crescent, through Thatto Heath Park, over the railway bridge, past the allotments and go to school. It was a journey full of temptations. It often took us a long time to get home after school. The park had a lake and swings; there was a possible diversion round a reservoir that we called a 'dam' and then there were shops to visit where we bought liquorices and 'Spanish' and penny lollies of the most hideously bright lime green colour.

Life at school was tough by modern standards, though we enjoyed ourselves immensely. The Headmaster, Mr. Mills, was a rather remote but relatively benevolent figure. He was, for example, very worried when the post-war rationing of sweets ended. He was convinced we would all stuff ourselves!

His staff were outwardly rather grimmer. Audrey was in Mrs. Brown's, Miss Addison's and Mrs. Bone's classes. These were the top divisions academically for nobody thought of multi-ability teaching. Audrey and indeed everyone from those days remembered Miss Addison, known as 'Finny Addy' after a kind of smoked fish. We especially remembered her wielding her ruler very effectively. Audrey, with her well-developed sense of justice, hated those teachers who meted out unfair and over-severe punishments to some of the boys, but they had very big classes to deal with and a wide variety of pupils to teach, so perhaps a tough approach was understandable.

Lessons were very formal. We sat in rows of wooden desks each of which had a bench attached and an in-built hole for ink pots, just right for using our pens with nibs and just right, too, for the person behind to dip our plaits into. Both Audrey and I had long, tight plaits with bows on the end. Every morning we had Math, English and 'Scripture' as we called it—the equivalent of religious studies today. It was very much centred on stories from the King James' version of the Bible and proved an excellent background for anyone interested in English Literature. We did indeed learn a lot. We were encouraged to read and the compositions she wrote must have helped Audrey to begin her writing career. Our Math was well up to the standard of the Grammar School.

As well as the academic subjects, we had singing lessons, sewing and art. Art was taken by Mr. Cowley who was very fond of what he called 'flat washes'. Many of his pupils as adults could not see a sunset with trees and houses silhouetted against a brilliant sky without thinking of his lessons.

The men teachers had just come out of the services and though some entertained us with war stories, they must have been affected mentally and physically by their experiences. In fact, although we were at primary school between 1945 and 1950, the Second World War still cast its shadow. Food was rationed very severely, even bread, and school dinners, a life-saver to many, were awful except for the good old British puddings and custard.

The best food in Lancashire in those days was certainly to be found at tea. 'Tea' was not the afternoon variety of the South of England but a major meal. On special occasions, Mrs. Gleave, Audrey's mother, provided excellent teas: sandwiches, cakes, scones, ham, salad and fruit and cream when you could get it.

I spent a lot of time at Audrey's home in those days. Her mother had a shop where I remember she sold dresses. Behind the shop was their home. There we swapped books, played card games such as 'Happy Families', and were entertained by music at the piano. I have a memory of Audrey telling me her piano crossed the Atlantic four times! It was at home in Lugsmore Lane that her love of music began.

The Gleaves were a very cheerful, welcoming family with lots of uncles and aunts, some of them 'adopted'. We used to visit Aunt Evelyn who had a cake shop and a lovely neighbour, Mrs Glynn—a Belgian who had married an English soldier after the war. She seemed very glamorous and spoke excellent English with a Lancashire accent! She taught us to make huge paper flowers.

Another source of entertainment was Audrey's much loved dog, Bessie. She was of an indeterminate breed but most affectionate and we teased her dreadfully. If we said 'cats*sss*' with a cat-like hiss, she would tear out of the house, barking furiously and leaping up at the yard wall. Poor Bessie!

Audrey came out with us sometimes in our pre-war Ford. Southport was a favourite for its huge expanses of beach and sand dunes and its amusement park. Modern children would find it tame but we loved its slides, ghost train and one of those Halls of Mirrors where you are surrounded by weird and distorted images of yourself.

Audrey went on annual holidays to the seaside with her parents. I have an image of visiting her at home only to find her in the middle of a vast ironing session. The neat little cotton dresses young girls wore in those days were hanging all-round the room in preparation for the exodus to Lytham, the posher neighbourhood of Blackpool.

Our lives might seem limited, but in many ways they were superior to those of modern children. We had a freedom that would terrify parents today. We ran wild in Taylor Park—a splendid place with winding paths, open spaces and a boating lake. Audrey and I could row ourselves round this with ease. If we walked down a rocky sandstone path by the golf course, we came to Eccleston—then quite rural with a farm where we could buy ice-cream. We went to dancing classes and learned to swim at Boundary Road Baths. There the sexes were strictly segregated, the women inevitably being relegated to the smaller and shallower of the two 'plunges' as they were called. Fortunately it was also the warmer with steam rising exotically from the green water.

Audrey was a very good reader. Thatto Heath Library provided us with a steady supply of books and there were newspapers and magazines to read. Audrey and I had a good friend, Nora Birchall, who as an adult, claimed that this library was a major source of our education. But we were lucky; our parents bought us books as presents and school encouraged us to read. Audrey favoured adventure stories and was always a great source of the latest 'Biggles'.

She loved the cinema too. We often went to 'the pictures' together. These expeditions were followed by heated discussions though sometimes as we grew older they could revolve more around the relative merits of the male stars than the cinema as art! I record in my diary in about 1953: 'Yesterday I went to the pictures with Audrey to see "Ten Tall Men". Audrey thinks Burt Lancaster is marvellous.'

Television, however, had its inevitable impact. The Gleaves had one in time for the 1953 Coronation and invited people to watch the event on the small black and white screen. I was often invited round to watch the current favourite children's television series like 'Billy Bunter' and sometimes more surprising programs with a more lasting impact. In 1954, I record: 'Went to Audrey's. Very enjoyable play on T.V. "1984". Scared me stiff!'

Mr. Gleave was a deacon of Toll Bar Congregational Church. This church, now called The United Reformed, is very democratic in its structure and its beliefs. Its influence on us was profound, without our realizing it. In one way it provided us with quite a lively social life. In May, for example, all the churches held Whit Walks or processions with colourful banners and there were parties and 'socials' especially at important times like Christmas and the Church's Anniversary. We were often expected to join in a choir and perform poems as part of the celebrations. We completely took for granted in our younger days the set of values that the church as well as our parents gave to us—values of honesty, justice and service to others that remained with us for the rest of our lives, long after the customs and traditions had become a folk memory.

1950 was a turning point in our lives. It was then that we took the dreaded eleven-plus exam. that would determine our future. In the event we both were successful for going to grammar school, Cowley School for Girls. If you could have seen Audrey at that time, she would have been wearing a very new and smart dark green tunic, a pale green blouse, a blazer with a badge, a striped tie and a hat. Woe betides anyone seen without her hat!

As new girls we were all divided up alphabetically; so Audrey and I were no longer in the same class. Our lessons were short and taught by specialists. There were lots of homework but lots of laughs too. As we grew older, for example, we developed a subversive attitude to sport. Left out of hockey teams, we would play our own version of touch rugby—after all we did live in St Helens, home to one of the greatest of Rugby League teams. A favourite punishment meted out by the P.E. (Physical Education) staff was to make us do extra dancing. But this was no punishment at all. Everyone loved to dance: ballroom, country and after 1955 Bill Hayley, rock 'n roll.

In class we were all very well behaved but there were rather strange lapses. When a male teacher taught Audrey's French group, chaos followed. Order marks were a major punishment. These were written in a book kept in the staff-room. I remember Audrey's class trooping one by one through our Drama lesson in the hall to collect the order marks he gave out in desperation. Poor man—he only lasted a year, but Audrey never did quite like French after that.

History and Geography were two of her key subjects in the Sixth Form—again we can see the beginnings of her future interests. There were few opportunities for girls in those days. The academics were expected to become teachers; a few doctors (the medical schools took only 10% of women) and then there were openings as nurses and secretaries. It did mean, however, that there were a great many talented women in those jobs—Audrey was one of them.

If Wordsworth's line 'The child is father of the man' was applied to Audrey, I can see in these early years the adventurous spirit, the hospitable and lively nature, the open mind and spirit, the humour and the intelligence that would enable her to embrace new ways of life, new careers, to bring up a family and to write her books yet remain true to herself.

Once we left school our ways parted, though we never lost touch. I am proud to say I was her bridesmaid! The next chapter belongs to others.

Chapter 2.2

Memoirs of Wendy Humphries—Audrey's Closest Sheffield University Friend

A wonderful friend—a super person—much loved and sadly missed!

Where do I start? At the beginning.

Audrey and I first met at College in Sheffield in 1957. We seemed to gel immediately perhaps because we were both only children. She became the sister I never had. There were so many good times during College days including trips to the cinema, the local pub, sing-songs around the piano in the Music Room; late nights back from the City. I remember the hilarious time when we climbed back in through the window around midnight pushing and shoving each other in! Oh, the bruises and scraped knees!

Then there was the episode when we were all in the TV room eagerly waiting to watch Christian Barnard's first heart transplant—Mary, a fellow student, perched on the back of the settee—the first incision a great crash and Audrey and I administering first aid and water to the recumbent figure! How we laughed afterwards. Amongst many activities Audrey and I were soon visiting local churches and places of worship—all to do with Audrey's subject of study I seem to recall. It wasn't long before we began to hitchhike on occasions to Manchester and then catch a train to St Helens to visit Audrey's parents. I was always made very welcome and had some super conversations with them both. I began to look upon them as my other family. And then having got the hitching bug we would sometimes do the journey in the opposite direction to my home in Cleethorpes to see my parents. How adventurous we were!

College days were great times with all of us cider making in Mary's room. Apples probably still fermenting on the roof! Miss Clarke doing her rounds at lights out—then whispered meetings often in Audrey's room the furthest away from Miss Clarke's. Tennis before breakfast—ups and downs but always a shoulder to cry on.

And then came Rag Week at the University when six young men wanted to meet six young girls. Audrey's expertise as an artist came to the fore when she drew each of us in barrels and we sent it as a reply. I met Mick who became a great friend and saw more films in 18 months at many flea-ridden cinemas than I have ever seen since.

Soon Audrey met Anu and I felt very privileged to meet his

friends and learn about a totally different culture. Geography was my subject so I was pleased to become involved with Anu and his friends and learn more about India.

Audrey and I continued to hitchhike and spread our trips further afield.
We had a very momentous holiday hitching down to London—couldn't escape quickly enough from the amorous advances of two lads in a lorry on the Guildford Bypass—continued on to Oxford and then eventually back up North.

Then came Audrey's 21st birthday—what a smashing time! I vividly remember bedtime shrieks from Audrey: "There's a spider in my bed!" To the rescue, poor little thing. How on earth was Audrey going to cope in India? At the end of the weekend I went home only to be mugged on the way from the bus stop to my house. Definitely a weekend to remember!

Then came Audrey and Anu's wedding. What a lovely affair! All of us college friends glammed up with our hats, stiletto heels, handbags, gloves and smart clothes. I seem to remember making myself a pale blue duster coat. What a lovely photo I have of the event; the bride looked stunning. And then a correspondence course followed when Audrey and Anu moved to India. Masses of letters changed hands; one in particular I remember when Audrey had to stop writing to call their servant to come and kill a large creepy crawly! THAT'S HOW SHE COPED WITH SPIDERS ETC!

Eventually Audrey, Anu and the children moved back to England. By this time I was living in a vicarage in West London with my husband Frank and our two children. Anu came to live with us for several weeks whilst Audrey was in St Helens with the children. Eventually Anu found a home for them in Hendon, North London, and we all met up once more.

Throughout we have kept in touch. Frank and I moved to Wembley. Audrey and Anu to Colindale, North London. Then Frank became ill but we did manage to get to Neil's (their son's) wedding reception in London.

What a super affair and how wonderful to meet up with old college friends!

Then followed a considerable time whilst I was nursing Frank at home after his long stay in hospital. When he died in 2007, I was finding it very difficult to come to terms with life. I spoke to Audrey and Anu in Sutton Coldfield where they had a house and eventually went to visit them. This was the beginning of my recovery. We had a great few days; talked endlessly and visited Birmingham. They showed me the sights and it was like old times. Audrey was not too well even then but she was still the same loving and kindly girl that I first met all those years ago.

When I left Anu suggested that I might like to join them on a cruise to the Baltic the following year and sit with them for dinner. What a great time we had. I'm only sorry that Audrey was not well enough to visit all the places ashore but it was so good to be with them both.

SUCH A WONDERFUL FRIEND, AUDREY—WE MISS YOU MUCH. MAY YOU REST IN PEACE!

Chapter 2.3

Memoirs of Mary Stephenson (née Kimberley): Another Sheffield Friend

Top North East Corridor, Collegiate Hall, Sheffield was the new address of six innocent young girls –Audrey, Chris, Doris, Judith, Mary and Wendy in September 1957. They were the product of Northern Grammar Schools and beginning to train as teachers.

Audrey's room was on the right as you faced the bathrooms and mine was close by, also on the right. We six all became friends very quickly as the initial shyness wore off. You had a special affinity with these new companions from your corridor and they became our term time family. The six of us walked to lectures en masse, in pairs or in little groups and hurried down the echoing stone staircase when the bell went for meals to eat at the Top North East table in the dining room.

I was surprised by the amount of salt Audrey sprinkled on savoury food, a habit she retained in later years. At college we took it in turns to sit at the head of the table and serve the twelve diners (six second-year and six first-year students) from the big main course and pudding dishes. Audrey was someone who soon learnt to calculate portion sizes and serve quickly to make sure the food stayed hot. Other people, including me, were glad when it wasn't their turn to serve out. I saw this practical bent of mind in later years when Audrey was our guest. She noticed that I had a bad back. We had a fine crop of weeds in the garden and whilst I was cooking she took the opportunity to do some weeding. One of our garden chairs had a wobbly arm and unfortunately this was the one Anu chose to use. Audrey discreetly alerted him to this defect so that he wouldn't have an accident and I wouldn't feel guilty of having duff garden furniture.

Our college bedrooms had dark green stained furniture and wooden panelled walls which didn't reach the ceiling. So our rooms could more accurately be described as cubicles. You could call out to your friends in a companionable way and if someone on the corridor talked in their sleep or had a nightmare all the girls heard. We used to gather in each other's rooms and drink milky coffee and nibble biscuits. Audrey loved to eat oranges but only if they had been peeled by someone else. Anu tells me that Audrey told him that her dad always peeled her oranges for her when she was little which she became used to in later years. She wasn't shy to ask us and I became an adept orange peeler as we chatted in her room. Being tidy was not her strong suit. Things were strewn across every surface of her bedroom; but in later years when my husband and I stayed at her home in Sutton Coldfield in England, it was a model of neatness.

Audrey, together with the other Top North East girls quickly adapted to the College custom of calling the lavatory 'Sc'. We were bemused by this term until it was explained to us that Sc was allegedly short for Scarborough, Queen of the Watering Places in England. "Just going to Sc" was a cry that echoed on the landing before we trooped down to lectures or caught the bus into town. The familiar word 'loo' was not widely used at that time.

Audrey and I must have been stalwarts of our local public libraries. We had both read lots of children's classics and also the *Lone Pine* books by Malcolm Saville which were set in Shropshire. (Audrey's daughter and son-in-law would later go on to buy a country house in that district). We had both been educated by Lancashire County Council and had learnt traditional folk songs and melodies at school. Her repertoire of songs and melodies was immense and I remember learning new ones from her, such as 'Farewell Manchester', Bonnie Prince Charlie's lament when leaving Manchester during the Jacobite rebellion. She also knew lots of jolly songs and introduced me to 'Nellie the Elephant', a song which always reminds me of her.

She was proud of her roots in a Northern Manufacturing town and knew a lot about glass making because St Helens is famous for glass and her dad worked at United Glass Bottles (UGB). She was keenly interested in Rugby League.

Audrey's pale skin and fair hair made her appearance

notable. Her lovely long hair was never worn down but always tied back in a ponytail or dexterously put up in a pleat or bun. People could fit into my clothes and people at College wondered about the ownership of one particular chestnut coloured dress with a black fur trim which we both liked and which we both wore frequently.

On one memorable occasion for a succession of warm summer nights we were serenaded by a group of Italian young men who stood on the pavement ('sidewalk' in America) looking up at the windows of Collegiate Hall. They must have known it was a girls' Hall of Residence. We were half asleep in bed when they first began to sing. Thrilled by this unexpected treat, we hung out of the windows in our nightdresses listening to 'Volare', 'Coma Prima', 'Que Sera', and 'Buena Sera Signorina', which later became familiar to the British public through a television advertisement as the Walls Ice Cream song, also featured. In between the songs we waved and clapped. Audrey was in fine voice as we gradually became brave enough to join in the choruses. After a while the boys gave us a cheer and walked on whilst we retired to bed giggling at this unforeseen event. When on the following two nights the concert was repeated we were in seventh heaven. It was like something in the theatre or a movie. It was not like Romeo and Juliet; there was no meeting and no passion, but it was a romantic and heart fluttering experience for artless young girls. When on the fourth night, by now the eagerly awaited event did not take place we were devastated!

Towards the end of our first year, Mr. & Mrs. Gleave— Audrey's parents—came to Sheffield to attend the College Open Day for parents and friends. As part of the entertainment we were putting on a display of creative or natural dancing, a phrase which we abbreviated to natty. We had bare feet and short blue tunics with matching knickers. Our presentation was done to the music of a mazurka by Chopin. It was wild and energetic and Audrey had to secure her pleat with extra hair pins. We cavorted about feeling very silly under the eagle eye of Miss Turner the PE Lecturer. We dare not look at each other and the audience only just managed to keep straight faces. Audrey's mum and dad laughed as they congratulated us on our capers and I remember thinking what warm-hearted people they were. You felt almost like an extra daughter within half an hour of meeting them. Later contacts with Ernie and Zena Gleave only served to confirm the first favourable impression.

I don't remember a great deal about any studying that we did but the social life has stayed in my mind and heart.

Friday nights were set aside for going to the College Jazz Club. The student musicians were very accomplished. Jiving was all the rage and Audrey partnered girl friends and also boys from College. It was very informal. Audrey also danced on the landing near the bathrooms in Collegiate Hall and in the corridor between the bedrooms. Records by the Shadows, Lonnie Donegan and Paul Anka were often on the turntable.

Almost every week we went to the movies. It only took about ten minutes to walk to the local cinema. Audrey accompanied us when we went walking near Rivlin dam or Hathersage, local scenic spots at the weekend. On cold winter days it was such a pleasure at the end of one of these excursions to relax in the warmth of Collegiate Hall with a cup of hot tea and a plate of pikelets (Yorkshire style crumpets) and Wet Nellies (drop scones).

The kitchen staff didn't try very hard with food at the weekend as many students went home. Salads were frequent even in winter. There were so many joyful times. We gathered round the Common Room piano and sang whilst Wendy played selections from Salad Days. We at times went for a meal to a Chinese restaurant called The Rickshaw where the ceiling was painted dark blue and was made of egg cartons. An Indian restaurant we used to go to had its walls covered in red flock wallpaper.

Those were happy years and the pleasant memories they evoke of good friends like Audrey will always be there to warm the heart of Mary Kimberley.

Chapter 2.4

Memoirs of Jenny Grixti –
Audrey's Fellow Teacher

Singlegate First School in Colliers Wood, South London, enjoyed a rich and varied mix of pupils from around the commonwealth and was therefore entitled to a teacher under "Section 11". Such a teacher would work in the classroom, with a group of students, alongside the class teacher, to help them integrate seamlessly into the culture in which they found themselves.

My class, vertically grouped from seven to nine year olds, prior to the constraints of a national curriculum, awaited our new teacher with eager expectancy. We were not to be disappointed.

When Mrs. Audrey Sanyal swept into our classroom she commanded instant respect. Like a ship in full sail, with her luxuriant blonde hair piled on top of her head, her imperious gaze encompassed each and every one of us. She silently settled at a table and motioned for a few fortunate ones to join her group.

She would speak with each gently and firmly, so that even the naughty ones were held in thrall. They would all work together to make puppets and put on puppet shows, including languages and artefacts from many cultures, always positive and encouraging; everyone wanted to be included in Mrs. Sanyal's group.

Audrey would accompany us on our visits to the farm or the Houses of Parliament; always a calm, steadying influence on the more high spirited children and a kind encouragement for the timid ones.

Gradually I came to know Audrey as a friend as well as a valued colleague and enjoyed her dry sense of humour, her artistry, musicality and flair. For example, on special occasions in the staff room, Audrey would put her own words to well-known tunes and we would all join in a serenade to the chosen individual to make it a special occasion they would never forget. Her acute perception of their individual idiosyncrasies was legendary.

She often spoke of her family and we particularly enjoyed hearing the exploits of Arjun, her first grandson. He was only three or four years old at that time but we have followed his achievements with interest. Now he is married to Charlotte, his childhood sweetheart. My husband Tito and I wish them every happiness and believe that the blessings and love bestowed on them by such dear grandparents will give them strength in their life together.

Although she always seemed calm and totally in control of the situation, Audrey did admit to not being comfortable with travelling on the Underground from North London everyday so it was with some relief that she moved to Morden in South London where some of her colleagues came to visit. Beth, one of our fellow colleagues, enjoyed helping Audrey with the garden.

Audrey and her husband Anu would come to our new year's parties when we lived in Mitcham. We were devastated when she announced that they were to go to live in Ohio. Audrey sent the children a wonderful letter, all about life in America, including photos of the icicles on the plants in her garden and description of the snowfall. All of this was so exciting for the children of our school. She had an instinctive knack of knowing just what would grab their attention.

We kept in touch after she left for America and were honoured to be invited to the reception at the Langham Hilton, London, to celebrate the marriage of their son Neil with Shomita. Several other colleagues were also invited. It was a magnificent reunion over which Audrey presided with her customary regal presence.

We were thrilled when Audrey and Anu visited us at our seaside bungalow in Sussex where we enjoyed some lovely outings. We also came to Sutton Coldfield near Birmingham where they had a house when we were shown the highlights of Birmingham. We enjoyed Audrey's surprise 70th birthday party where we were treated to a room at the local Holiday Inn. It was a privilege to meet all her family and friends. Everyone got on really well. Although it was a surprise, when Audrey walked in, seeing everybody there, she managed her usual majestic composure. Her delight and obvious pleasure and love for her family were a joy to behold.

Thank you, Audrey, for enriching all our lives. A great presence hugely missed!

Thanks for the memories!

Chapter 2.5

Memoirs of Santimoy
(Audrey's Brother-in-law)

I met her in1961 when my brother brought Audrey, his newly married wife, to Calcutta (now Kolkata) from London. We enjoyed their marriage ceremony according to Hindu rites in Kolkata. All our family members came to attend the function.

Everyone loved her for her extraordinary polite behaviour. She loved me like her brother. She told me about her parents. We soon became very good friends. She respected my parents very much. My mum and dad also treated her like their daughter.

During my father's severe heart attack she tried her best to resuscitate him. Despite her best efforts my father died.

She had many good qualities. We grew up in an extended family of 20 cousins in Howrah, a suburb of Kolkata. She lived in Gomia, Bihar for some ten years with my brother as he worked there. They lived in a very nice bungalow (a ranch style house). When they visited us at Howrah, she mingled very freely with all of our relatives. She started speaking Bengali (our mother tongue) and picked it up very quickly. She was serious about learning our language and soon reached a standard when she could speak Bengali for hours. She wore sari all the time. She learned to cook Bengali dishes within a short span. She loved Indian songs and could sing a few.

My wife and I visited her house in India, London and also in the USA with our children. She gave us a rousing welcome every time. I have never seen her being rude to anybody. She was like a Goddess to us. My wife Rupa and I as well as our children loved and respected her very much. I took many pictures of her. She always praised the quality of my photos.

During her first (and last) visit to my son's house in Toronto from Florida at the time of the birth of his second child, she went to see the baby late at night even after a long plane journey earlier that day.

While I am writing this, my granddaughter Tari told me to write her feelings for Audrey that she also misses her very much.

We celebrated her birthday at Toronto which regrettably turned out to be her last birthday!

We miss her very badly. She was my brother's best friend.

Actually they were made for each other.

May her soul rest in peace!

Chapter 2.6

Memoirs of Shanta Panesar (our daughter)

Ma

What do I say about my mum, known as Ma in our family? She was so full of grace and so caring. She was softly spoken and kind always. I never remember her raising her voice to Neil, my brother, nor myself. She was the same with our father. My children, Arjun, Amar and Harkrishan also remember her gracious and wonderful presence. This way of conducting herself was the same when it came to her son-in-law, Dav and her daughter-in-law, Shomita, and everyone else she came across in her life.

She lived a life of a queen in India, England and America.

She followed her creative pursuits actively, having worked only 16 years of her life as a schoolteacher in England. In India she took part in a drama club, acting in several productions. She also directed and produced several nativity plays for children, roping her own children into several parts. She wrote two books and numerous poems. The first book she published was *Talavera*. She in fact emailed the publishers the okay to print the second book, *Naseby*, in the trilogy she intended to write, the day before she passed away!

She loved to paint and play the piano and sing. My first musical memories are of her singing: 'Hathi Mera Sathi', or my friend the elephant! Her other favourites were 'Yellow River' by Christie, 'Obla di Obla Da' by the Beatles and 'Sea Cruise' by Herman's Hermits. She not only sang in English but learnt many Bengali songs phonetically when she went to live in India, 50 years ago. She learnt my father's language Bengali within a year of marriage, always wore a sari and learnt to cook Indian food whilst living in India. She approached everyone equally, making time for anyone, whatever their status or station in life.

She never gossiped or talked ill of anyone. If anyone was untoward or unkind, she would just step aside. Amazingly she never got bored. She was so self-contained. Often I would ask her, "Ma, do you really never get bored?" And she would reply, "Never." She would add: "I don't know why, but I never get bored."

When Ma was at the hospital, from 2- 27 October 2010, Harkrishan (my youngest son) asked Ma, "Have you not got bored there?" and she responded, "Not at all."

They say all you are is what you are because of your parents. The phrase "love on legs" sums up her parents which sums Ma up.

She was with me during each birth of her three grandchildren, and she conducted herself as if she were having a cup of tea. She showed no signs of concern or worry on her face, because she knew that would worry me. After Harkrishan (our youngest) was born, I pleaded with her, "Ma, please hold him as I don't want to drop him as I have been up for 36 hours." She looked at me aghast and said, "Shanta, you have been up for 36 hours. So have I!" So we placed Harkrishan in the "fish" tank next to the hospital bed.

In the last five weeks of borrowed time with her, I had the amazing opportunity of spending some wonderful moments with her. Within a week after her operation she started to improve. If someone had said you have only four weeks with your mum, that's how I would have spent them, as we did. Each moment with her was intense; we told each other we loved each other. I would kiss her all over her face. She would kiss my cheeks and stroke my face.

She filled me up with so much love, the love which will now have to last me my lifetime. On the Friday before she passed away, the last time I saw her, she was so radiant, shining, full of life and overflowing with love. We laughed and joked and did a crossword puzzle together. Harkrishan shouting out the clues and Amar (my second son), Ma and I shouting out loud the answers. I asked Harkrishan, "Shall we take the crossword book home?" He said, "No, we'll do another one with Ma when we come next time." Ma turned round to me and said, "I won't need the crossword book." Did she have the premonition of her death? Who knows?

Ma was an asset. Such a wonder. Such an enigma. She was dignified. Her son-in-law poignantly describes her as carrying the dignity of England. She was majestic, noble, holding herself together whatever the circumstances, coping impeccably. Our father was so lucky to have an amazing wife like her. We were very lucky to have a mother as her. My husband Dav and sister-in-law Shomita were very lucky to have a mother- in-law like her and Arjun, Amar and Harkrishan (our sons) were very fortunate to have a gran like her. To add to that, she left me the gift of the intense love we shared in the last four weeks. She could not sleep for the first week at hospital as she was having nightmares of dying. Upon doing a Sikh (my religion) prayer called Kirtan Sohila which stops nightmares, she was not scared and started doing well. Not only did that lift her fear of dying in nightmares, it lifted her fear of dying per se.

Ma, Audrey Carole Sanyal, née Gleave, was a golden wonder, a gracious, a kind, loving trouper. Ma, we will always love you. We will always remember you as that fun-loving, kind and amazing woman. May existence, Christ and the Guru hold you in a close embrace as we do in our hearts.

Ma had a Christian service, as she had lived in Christ consciousness. We decided that we were going to take Ma's ashes to scatter in the Ganges to reflect her connection with India and it also proved so essential in letting go of her. We first went to Calcutta, my Dad's birthplace and where many of his family still reside, arriving on December 2, 2010. On December 3 my brother scattered Ma's ashes in the Ganges. It felt like the right thing to do; it felt that she was free, moving from womb to womb.

December 4, 2010 involved feeding my Dad's relatives in Calcutta which was very necessary for my dad in particular, to know that he has a huge family who cared so much. It was also important for everyone in India, who knew her, to share their feelings about her and to grieve collectively. It was also vital for me to meet the beloved ones, aunts, who looked after me and loved me seamlessly when I was young. I also realized I still have someone I can call Ma, my Aunt, my dad's only brother's wife, who I have always called Chotoma or little mother. As I used to call my mum Ma, it was very important for me to know I can still call someone Ma.

On December 5, 2010 we went to an ashram where my Uncle's and Aunt's spiritual guide has opened a school and residence for orphans. He was a very smiley Guru and it was a privilege to be in his presence. The next day we went to Amritsar. I cried all the way round the prakarma, around the Golden Temple itself. I asked the Guru, existence, to look after Ma's soul forever before placing the rumala, an ornate cloth placed on the Guru Granth Sahib.

On December 7, we went to Dav's ancestral pind, where three of his ancestors became shaheed, or went to their martyrdom 300 years ago. That day was Ma's birthday and I was crying a lot. Another Babaji there asked me: "Do you want to be close to the Guru?" I said, "Yes." He went on to ask me: "Do you do paat" (recitation of hymns from the Sikh scriptures) and I answered in the affirmative. He asked specifically what, and I answered him. He then went on to say: "If you do paat and wish to be close to your guru then you need to see life and death in the same way."

He then asked me to make a promise to him and I agreed. He said: "Promise you will leave your grief here." For some unknown reason I agreed! He explained that Ma had completed her responsibilities here and had moved on to another life. He continued, "So, what are you crying for?"

He also spoke about those who die with their mouths open, as Ma did. He said that those who die with their mouths open need another human life before they are mukhti (achieve *Nirvana*). He took about an hour explaining such things to me for which I am very grateful. It felt that the bulk of the grief had been left at the feet of the shaheed babbe, the Sikh martyrs, at the place where they fell.

The next day, we went to see another Babaji, Baba Arjun Singh, who said that Ma's soul is at peace. The following day we went to Baba Bakalle to offer a rumala and to see Baba Makhan Singh, the Babaji there, but he was elsewhere. We met some Nihang Singhs there. Then we spent most of the time at Amritsar airport, six hours to be precise, waiting for our delayed plane. We spent a night in the Sri Nanak hotel in Delhi and then we were on the flight back to England the next day.

One thing that has become concrete in my mind is that Nanak's naam is essential in life, death and during the passage of the soul from one life form to the next.

Chapter 2.7

Memoirs of Shomita Maitra
(our daughter-in-law)

Regretfully, I did not have the opportunity to spend much time with Ma and get to know her very well. But from the moment we met, I felt her wisdom and her kindness. She showered those around her with unconditional love. She accepted me into her family with open arms, laughed with me during good times and comforted me during the not so good ones. We had some really nice chats at our kitchen table over a few glasses of white wine and plain (no flavours other than Salt and Vinegar!) crisps.

I am amazed at how she seemed to meet all of life's challenges with strength and grace. It takes a remarkable personality to be able to travel halfway across the world to a place and language completely unknown to start a newly married life. It takes an even more remarkable one to be able to adapt to one's new surroundings, actually learn the language and be accepted into a family with a completely different cultural heritage.

Despite being immersed in a culture and ways foreign to her for many years, Ma was able to keep her individuality and British heritage very much alive. She was always an avid reader and accomplished actress, and more recently a published writer. I understand that she both directed and acted in many plays while in India (although her son insists that his acting career was brought to a grinding halt when Ma kept him home when he had chicken pox and he missed his big acting break as the leading man of the play!). We spent many hours watching one of our favourite actors, Sean Bean, in the Sharpe series. It always makes me laugh when I think of how Ma then went to the library in Lakeland, their Florida home, and made them order the entire series for her!

I remember how disappointed she was at the small part she was given in the Christmas Murder Mystery in Connecticut— we thought that we were sparing her since she had just arrived from Birmingham, England that day but didn't factor in the fact that her passion for acting would override her jet lag!

At our wedding, Ma and Neil danced to the lyrics of 'Forever Young'. I was struck by how true some of the words seemed—and how they reflect the ideas and values that I always think Ma must have instilled in her children and grandchildren.

May you grow up to be righteous
May you grow up to be true
May you always know the truth
And see the lights surrounding you
May you always be courageous
Stand upright and be strong
May you stay forever young

May your hands always be busy
May your feet always be swift
May you have a strong foundation
When the winds of changes shift
May your heart always be joyful
And may your song always be sung
May you stay forever young

I think Ma would want us always to celebrate her life and not grieve over our loss even though a place is vacant in our hearts.

We will never forget you Ma, and may your heart always be joyful wherever you are out there looking out over and after us.

Chapter 2.8

Memoirs of Nilamber (Neil) Sanyal (our son)

When I picture my mother I always see her smiling and talking about some of her favourite things and past times. She loved reading, history, languages, music, the theatre, comedy, puzzles, crosswords, the odd glass of red wine and conversation. She did not like cooking although she was good at it. In spite of her saying she didn't like travelling she lived in three continents and moved residence some twenty times! In addition my parents annually visited my sister in the UK, me in Connecticut from Florida.

Wherever she went, she seemingly effortlessly embraced the culture and the traditions, made friends and flourished.

I am still amazed as to how as a just-married young woman in 1961, she left her country, her friends and parents to travel several thousand long miles to go to India and very soon had truly made this her home—having learnt the language, how to cook and eat the food, and how to conduct herself within all the very different nuanced social mores.

She was always an advocate for the underdog, the downtrodden, cared about the less fortunate and would passionately speak up about injustice wherever she observed it.

I was amazed at some of the things that she'd accomplished but didn't think much of. She started her teaching career in one of the roughest working class blue collar areas of North England—took this all in her stride and thrived! Also as a teacher in London, for over a year, she had a two and a half hour round trip daily commute—there were never any complaints. It was only after she came to the US that she let on that she was thrilled to be a lady of leisure!

A lot of my favourite things and vital aspects of my personality I inherited from her: my love of music, history, literature, appreciation for the surreal, my sense of humour, my optimism, my beliefs and political sensibilities. She was my friend, we had a marvellous effortless and fun relationship and I discussed most things with her. With my mother I always felt much loved and that there was nothing she wouldn't do for me.

My mother was a fair lady. When I was about seven we lived in India and my mother was a part-time English teacher at the school I was in. I hadn't done too well and thought I'd sneak out early from my math's test and who should I meet as I quietly stepped outside the exam. classroom but my mother—caught red handed! She immediately ordered me back into the classroom; spoke to my math's teacher and ensured I answered every question on the test! So much for expecting any special favours from my mum!

Naturally she was the best mum in the world.

In India between the ages of 9 and 11, I went to a boy's boarding school. Every week all the boys would write a postcard home to their parents. One week for want of anything better to write, and obviously needing some attention, I lamented as to how I had holes in my shoes from having walked so much and that I was hungry for not having been adequately fed at school. The food and the lack thereof was a gross exaggeration but I do remember having holes in my shoes! Needless to say (and I was pretty sure this would occur) I rapidly received money for new shoes and a large amount of "tuck"—cakes (madeleine cakes that my Mum had made—I still remember how delicious they tasted!), biscuits and the like, which made me the envy of my fellow boarding school friends and inmates!

She opened my ears to wonderful music at an early age. The Beatles, Bread, Herman's Hermits and Trini Lopez are some of the first songs I heard, loved and still enjoy. I also remember at the age of eight being trusted to use the record player and quickly mastering the delicate art of placing the needle on the record without scratching it! Some of these LP's survived an eight-year-old child's attention and still exist in our collection.

She had a "no nonsense" sense about her and in my youth whenever I was bemoaning some imagined hardship or chore—she'd tell me to "pull up my socks", stop complaining and to get on with it. She was a walking encyclopaedia, my very own Google, and when she was around if I had questions about history or some other subject—I'd always ask her first and marvel at her breadth of knowledge and her answers. At Christmas time when we played board games such as Trivial Pursuit, everyone wanted to be on her team as we all knew she'd carry the team to victory!

My mother had a wonderful time at Highland Fairways, Lakeland, Florida, our parents' winter home. She was always mentioning the Red Hat ladies, her tenure as queen, delighting in the numerous fun escapades of the Red Hat ladies, her poetry writing and recitals, singing in the choir and all the other great social activities and occasions at Highland Fairways. She was always tickled and amused as to how because she was from England, that a lot of her friends would ask her detailed questions about the English royal family—assuming that she had a personal active hotline directly to the queen of England!

Chapter 2.9

Tribute by Tarun Maitra—our Nephew

It was a Sunday morning when as usual I was talking to Auntie Audrey and Uncle Anupam. They were in Sutton Coldfield, England and we were in LA, California.

No matter whether they were in Florida or England, we used to talk to each other almost every Sunday.

That Sunday she was asking me about my daughter's marriage in India that they were coming to attend a month or so later.

It was around 2.30 p.m. LA time on 31 October 2010, when I got a text message: "MA DEAD BABA" (dad in Bengali). I was very confused. I didn't understand and called Soma my wife; she was equally confused as we both had lost our dads years ago; who, then, is this baba? (Uncle Anupam copied me this text to his son Neil). Two hours later I got a call from Neil from Connecticut who confirmed the devastating news.

How could it be possible? Only a few hours back I was talking with her.

She was the dearest member of all our family and especially to me.

Since my schooldays in the 60s, I had visited her several times in India, England and Florida.

When we were in school in Tatanagar, some 90 miles from Gomia, Bihar, where my Uncle used to work, they used to come to pick me and my sister up during summer holidays. We used to look forward to the annual event being pampered by Auntie Audrey.

She was a soft spoken lady with a very big heart.

To our family she was an angel!

When they used to live in England, they had come to visit us (my mother was Uncle's sister) in Tatanagar and were going back. We had to come to see them off at the airport. Soon after they had boarded the plane, my Uncle found her crying! He was perplexed as to why she would suddenly start crying. Did she have any sudden health problems? Auntie Audrey told Uncle that she couldn't stop crying as she was going to miss us so much!

She was kind to everybody.

One of my cousins used to live in a rental property in

Kolkata and had a problem with the owner. She resolved this at one stroke – she bought him a house!

She used to take part in every function in our family no matter how sick she was.

I remember during our marriage in LA, since my mum from India couldn't attend, she did everything required by the groom's mother at a Bengali wedding.

My wife Soma and I were very special to her.

Once after visiting us at LA, she wrote us a letter from Florida which we treasure with immense love and gratitude.

The letter gave us a glimpse into her feelings—as to how much she loved us.

She had her last Christmas with us in 2009 in LA. Before the Christmas dinner she read out a poem she wrote about us which is one of our precious possessions.

I don't think she is not with us; rather, she is with us all the time.

Chapter 2.10

Tribute by Anurupa Sanyal—Audrey's sister-in-law

I am the wife of Santimoy Sanyal—only brother of Audrey's husband, Dr. Anupam Sanyal.

One should write about her and tell others about Audrey, for she was such an unusual person.

Here is my attempt to share my thoughts with the readers about her.

She, an English lady, married a Bengalee and completely integrated herself in Bengali culture.

Those who never knew her or met her would be surprised to know that she was more of a Bengalee than some of the present-day Bengalese ladies.

When she visited our house (we lived in an extended family) in Howrah (near Calcutta), she used to speak to every member of the family, young or old, in fluent Bengali.

I was married 11 August in 1967. She was visiting her parents in England with her children then and came back, I think, in December. I had heard so much about her from members of our family and was dying to meet her. That day arrived. We all went to receive them at the railway station. I was very excited, waiting for the moment. I was very surprised to see a memsahib (a Caucasian) in sari, who is a member of our family, with two very pretty children aged 5 and 3.

To her I was a new member of the family. She came forward and gave me a big hug! This was my first meeting with her.

I was in for another surprise. After she came back to our house, the first thing she did was to touch the feet of all the elders (an Indian custom of showing respect to elders) and there were quite a few of them. She came to know about this custom from her husband and followed it without being prompted to do so. She also hugged and kissed each of the younger ones.

After they went back to Anu's place of work in Gomia, Bihar, I used to count the days for my next meeting with her and talk to my friends about this amazing sister-in-law of mine. Indeed, I used to address her as my sister.

My husband and I visited them in Gomia a few months later. I have very happy memories of those days when she couldn't do enough for us. I have fond memories of the days when they used to visit us in Calcutta.

When my nephew Neil and niece Shanta were little, she used to send them during their vacation to stay with us. I was so pleased to have them and they loved me dearly and address me as 'Chotoma'(Younger Mother). My husband had quite a few cousins. They also loved to have them. My in-laws (their grandparents) and all of us used to have very happy times together.

One anecdote sticks out in my mind. She came to attend the wedding of one of the cousins. We were all so surprised and impressed to see how she joined all the ladies in observing the Bengali wedding rites including blowing a conch shell—an Indian custom to celebrate an auspicious occasion. Even now when those cousins and we get together we reminisce about those days and Audrey's inimitable interest in being one of us.

All families have good and bad times including the demise of members. She not only came forward with genuine words of condolences but also saw to it that the unfortunate widow did not suffer from hardship.

She could not attend our daughter Sudeshna's wedding but was present at the marriage of our son Saswata. We welcomed them at Calcutta airport with garlands. To be able to do so was one of the happiest memories of my life.

She received Shalini our new daughter-in-law on her first arrival in our house in a ceremony that is traditional for a Bengali wedding. The professional way she conducted it surprised all.

Our 'Guru' (religious mentor) visited us to bless the bride.

Audrey was not at all well that day. We didn't expect her to come to pay her respects to him. We were very astonished and touched when she arrived in a sari (which she mostly wore in India) with her head covered and touched the feet of our Guru.

My daughter and her husband Biswaroop invited her to their house during her stay in Calcutta, an invitation she readily accepted which pleased us to no end. Their daughter Totini was very surprised to see a Caucasian woman in a sari speaking fluent Bengali! All of them liked her very much.

She came to our house in Calcutta a few times from England and America. She used to tell me that she felt most comfortable during her stay with us as she found our house the cleanest of all the Indian houses she visited.

We visited them in London with my mother-in-law. We have very happy memories of our stay when we saw her first grandson Arjun, my mother-in-law's first great grandson.

We also visited them in Naperville, Illinois, during the wedding of her son Neil. I was honoured to receive Shomita her daughter-in-law in the ceremonial way that a new daughter-in-law is received in the groom's house for the first time. She asked me to do this and I was delighted to carry out all the traditional Bengali wedding rites that she left to me to do.

My husband and I visited her and my brother-in-law at their house in Lakeland, Florida in 2006. They looked after us so well that I was in tears when leaving them.

Our first grandson Souryya was born in Toronto on 1 May

2010 around midnight. Audrey and Anu arrived in Toronto from Tampa, the same day around 7 in the evening. She invited herself to join us to see the newborn after such a long flight. When the baby arrived home from the hospital, she welcomed the baby by blowing a conch shell, an Indian custom to celebrate a happy event. She used to spend a good deal of her time with the baby on her lap. These are happy memories now. She added her choice of name— Bikram, meaning strong—to his first name Souryya.

Shree, our first grandchild, also met her for the first time and she loved her. She, now 8, still talks about her.

Our son Saswata once gave Anu a surprise visit to Lakeland, Florida, on his birthday. Audrey was his 'partner in crime' in arranging the visit.

We celebrated their 49th wedding anniversary in Toronto on 6th May. Who knew that that would be their last one!

Nobody has everlasting peace and happiness, and God suddenly took her away from us on 31 October 2010. She left behind her husband of nearly 50 years, her children, their spouses and grandsons. Her husband, her children and their spouses, made a trip to Calcutta to scatter her ashes in the holy river Ganges.

May her soul rest in peace—that's all I pray for.

To quote the famous Indian poet Rabindranath Tagore: *Chokher jole laglo jowar dookher parabare Oh Chand!* (Oh Moon you brought a high tide of tears of sorrow).

Chapter 2.11

Memoirs of Anupam (Anu) Sanyal

I, Anu, met her on 17 January 1959 during her final year at Sheffield and had the privilege of her company as my life's partner till 31st October 2010.

This is a snapshot of our life together.

After the Going Down Ball (see Introduction), we went on seeing each other most Saturdays when we went to the pictures. Those days Gaumont Theatre was one of the popular ones in the City where we met at 7.30. We recalled our meetings many a time afterwards. "See you at 7.30 in front of Gaumont" brought back many memories!

Within the first month or two after we started seeing each other, I found myself enjoying her company more and more. She also saw me whenever I asked her unless she was busy with her studies.

Coming from an ultra-orthodox Bengali Hindu Brahmin family, any step towards a serious relationship with a Christian was out of the question. I realized that and told myself that this relationship had to be of a temporary nature. More so, Audrey was going back home in St Helens in July that year (1959) after completing her final exam. I perhaps kidded myself by thinking that would be that!

Nearer the Easter time, I asked her if she would be willing to hitchhike to Scotland with me during the Easter holidays. I was pleasantly surprised when she agreed. Hitchhiking in the 50s in England was very popular especially with the poor students and quite safe (Not now!!).

We started out from St Helens on 1 April, 1959. Our first port of call was Stranrear and then along the West coast via Girvan and Ayr to Coraith and then on to Loch Lomond until we finally reached Edinburgh. We went to Edinburgh Castle where we saw Audrey's Uncle Norman's name in the Book of Remembrance. He belonged to the Liverpool Scottish Regiment and was killed in WW1.We also visited the Zoo. We stayed at youth hostels every night. (There were separate wings for men and women). Got back to St Helens on the 7th April Hitchhiking both ways was uneventful, tiring but very enjoyable. The dates are correct as I found these in a pocket diary that Audrey, unknown to me, kept which I found last year amongst her papers. My budget was 5 Pounds (compare this with my weekly bursary of a little over 7 pounds). I still had some change left when we got back.

Amongst the many films that Audrey and I saw, before she

went back home in July 1959 after finishing her course, 'South Pacific' sticks out in my memory and I see that it also finds a notable mention in her diary; perhaps because of the love affair and marriage between the American Soldier and the Polynesian girl!

Going through her diary, I could make out that she was serious about our relationship by May; that is a little over five months after our first meeting and were discussing the possibility of marriage and envisioned the insurmountable problems that this would involve. Both felt very miserable but neither of us wanted to finish off. In fact, we planned to hitchhike to Paris and set off on Sunday 12 July, 1959 (as recorded in her diary), ferried across to Calais and hitchhiked along the Euro route. Stayed the night in a hotel in Abbarile. This was the first time we spent a night in the same room. There was only one bed. I lay on the carpet leaving the bed to Audrey. While I was trying to sleep, she told me she was afraid to sleep by herself. I reluctantly (yes, that's true!) joined her in the bed and said that the real reason was that she wanted me in bed with her! Next thing I knew was a smart slap which really hurt!! (She later told me she didn't remember it at all!).

Quite by coincidence, we arrived in Paris on 14 July, the Bastille Day. The fireworks display was spectacular! Saw the famous Mona Lisa and other paintings in the Louvre museum and other places of touristic interest like Notre Dame. Hitchhiked to Versailles and saw the magnificent palace. On our way back we didn't succeed to catch a lift to reach our next destination and was stuck at Alencon—a place middle of nowhere—no hotel! Spent the night in a field with the sky overhead! I was more concerned about my shoes which I tied to my sleeping bag! Our luck next morning was better. We reached Ille Besnard—a seaside place where we could get in the local youth hostel. It was boiling hot and swimming in the sea was a great relief. Next destination—Mont St Michel. No luck with lifts! Spent the night at a camping site. Next day we reached Mont St Michel. It was worth the trouble. A Castle and a Place of worship built into one. Audrey bought a doll.

Now our way back to England. Got to Caen on Wednesday 22 July and on to Abbarile. Found a room at the same hotel. No recurrence of the episode during our last stay! It was early evening by the time we arrived at Dover. We had a total of 10 shillings (50 Pence or 80 Cents) between us! Found out that there is a Truck Depot in the centre of London where one could get a ride to the North. By the time we arrived there (don't remember the name of that part of London), we were told that almost all trucks for the North had left. However, just one hadn't, the Office girl told us. When we approached the Truck Driver, his wife (he had gone out to buy sweets or cigarettes perhaps) agreed to take us, but not in the cabin. We had to sit on the empty trailer which had no roof! With no choice we sat in the middle of the trailer nearest to the back of the cabin and tightly held each other's hands as the trailer had no protective wall on the sides. As the truck veered, the trailer, attached to the cabin by a sling rod, also veered and one could fall off the trailer! The truck was going halfway to our destination and we had to get off at Crewe. It reached there in the early hours of the morning. It rained between London and Crewe and we got drenched. The truck pulled up at a Service Station. We tried to find a truck going north but didn't find one! So we started walking on the pitch dark road around 3 or 3.30 in the morning, thumbing for a lift. This time we got lucky soon after we started and a small van pulled up. It was going to Manchester from where we could catch a bus to St Helens. The lone driver agreed to take us! What a relief! Within seconds of getting in the van, we both fell asleep and woke up only when the van was just entering Manchester. The driver could have taken us anywhere and we would have had no idea as we were fast asleep. We never thought that something awful could happen to us. I don't think any young couple of today in sane mind would have done what we did without thinking of the possible consequences.

The ignorance of youth!

When we arrived at Audrey's parents' house, the first thing her mother said, which I still remember, is that we looked like we had come up from a coal mine! It was 25 July 1959.

I had a Greek friend at the University, called Emanuel Papadakis—a Captain in the Greek Army—doing a Master's degree under a NATO scholarship. His English was poor and somehow he took me to be his Tutor. He must have felt less shy to admit his language problem to me compared to the Fellow English students. We became very good friends—his wedding present to us still has pride of place in our Living Room Cabinet.

The question he asked me the first time he met me after I went back to the University from our trip to France stands out in my memory. Emanuel said, "You were away for almost two weeks; you must have slept with her?" A very personal question! I said that I didn't (which was true). He said that had I been anybody else he would not have believed me. As it was me, he did. But he said, "In that case you are either God or Impotent!!!" I said, "I am neither!"

136

Audrey started teaching on Monday 24 August 1959 (as recorded in her diary) in an Elementary school in St Helens.

We continued seeing each other. I would hitchhike from Sheffield to St Helens most Friday afternoons and take a train back on Monday morning. Most of our conversations centred round the improbability of our spending the rest of our life as man and wife.

This perhaps calls for an explanation.

Besides the obvious fact that we belonged to different faiths, in the Bengali Hindu family I came from, marriages were mostly arranged. One of my cousins was the first in the family to break the tradition by having a boy-meet-girl marriage. The girl came from the same locality and the families knew each other. The fact that they chose their spouses themselves caused a huge furore. In my case the problem was of a different magnitude altogether. I wanted to marry not only a Christian but also a Caucasian which was practically unknown in our society.

I didn't have much hope of receiving my parents' blessing. I however couldn't possibly stop seeing Audrey. I explained the whole situation to her in great detail: she didn't express any intent to break off. So we carried on seeing each other, falling in love deeper and deeper and realizing that it would be well-nigh impossible for me to marry somebody else, either in England or have an arranged marriage on my return to India.

My research work was reaching a critical stage with regards to the time limit and hence demanded my utmost attention;

I was going through quite a stressful period.

After I finished my studies and received my Ph.D., after consulting with Audrey and her parents, I wrote to my father a long letter in English. (I used to write to my mum and dad once a week in Bengali so that both could read as my mother couldn't read, write or speak much English). This was written in English so that only my father could read it and I left it to him to speak to my mother about Audrey. In the letter I gave as many details as possible about Audrey and her parents. I reiterated that her feelings towards me and her willingness to spend her life with me *in India* were not a result of an infatuation.

This letter was not a bombshell! Before I had written this letter, I had written in my weekly letters about her and that I had met her parents and how hospitable they were, etc. However, I was not surprised with the reply I received. My father was very much a realist and we had an atypical Indian father and son relationship. What does that mean to the Western readers?

An Indian son during our days in 1940s did whatever the father told (not asked) the son to do. He was not like that all. He knew his son and how much I loved him and mum. He trusted me and knew that I wouldn't do anything to hurt them. Our relationship was more like friends.

He wrote back to say that while he respected my feeling for Audrey and he believed it was a temporary one and more like infatuation for it would be very very difficult for a Caucasian woman to become a part of a Hindu Orthodox Bengali Family as we were. Also, most of these bi-racial marriages end up in failure, he wrote, especially those when the couples try to live in India. He left it to me, but was very apprehensive about my mother accepting the idea of an English daughter-in-law with whom she couldn't converse. He thought that it could be too much of a shock for her to bear.

If I did go ahead, he was convinced that I, with my Caucasian Christian wife, would have to live outside our society. I came from an extended family—too extended in fact, as my father and his four brothers with their wives and children lived under the same roof in a big house. My grandmother was the matriarch. We were 20 cousins!

I had by then received a good job in India. It provided housing which had all the creature comforts. The workplace, called Gomia in the state of Bihar, was 250 miles away from Calcutta (now Kolkata).

So staying with my parents wouldn't have arisen. Still, my parents could not accept the idea of having an English daughter-in-law.

Audrey's and my parents wrote to each other and after a prolonged period of correspondence, my father suggested that I should not get engaged. He suggested that I come back and discuss the issue with them as well as with the other members of my family. Audrey's parents told me that they would find it difficult to give us their blessings unless we receive my parents' blessings without which they felt that the marriage wouldn't work. (We however got engaged for which I had to buy her a ring, costing me some 3 weeks of my monthly scholarship money)! Her parents, however, always introduced me to their family as Audrey's boyfriend and not fiancé!

My father asked me not to write to my mother about my intent to marry an English girl and suggested that I tell her in person on my return.

By that time I had received my Ph.D. and waited for sailing back to India,

I continued to talk to Audrey about the rigours and the ways of life which were much different from what she had been used to. I deliberately painted a gloomy picture but she always looked at the bright side and said that unless she saw it she wouldn't have the real idea; but to her, marriage is only for once and she was prepared to make it work whatever it took. (She meant it and proved herself, much to my utter surprise throughout my life!). She never stopped amazing me with her steely determination to integrate herself into my society. Numerous examples flood back, but those for later.

I had to wait for some two months to catch the boat. During this time we went to Europe, not hitchhiking, for we were rich then as Audrey was teaching and my Professor very kindly kept my grant on! We looked up a friend in Aachen in Germany and also visited Cologne, Amsterdam, and Paris.

Audrey's parents told me as she was their only child, they would like to have the wedding in their church.

Their farewell talk to me was "come back with your parents' blessings. Don't come back if you don't get their support".

I sailed from Southampton on 1 September, 1960. I took an overnight sleeper from Liverpool. Audrey and her parents came to see me off at Liverpool Lime Street. The parting was very painful. Both of us howled and howled! I was afraid that it would probably the last time I would see her since I wasn't sure that I would be able to turn my parents' view around, and if I couldn't, our marriage without the support of either of our parents might not come off.

In the event I was wrong and very pleased to be wrong! Audrey however never thought that I wouldn't come back, as she told me later.

I arrived in Bombay on the 16th September. The sailing was rocky at times but I felt miserable all the time wondering about our future together.

My parents came to receive me at the Bombay Pier. I was delighted to see them after a lapse of over three years. We took the train to Howrah, a suburb of Calcutta—a journey for two nights, some 1200 miles!

Audrey was writing to me every day to the address of one of my Calcutta friends, as we lived in an extended family and everybody could see the post. Audrey was still unknown to the members of my family except my father and a cousin who knew and kept it a secret. Audrey wrote that she was praying for me and asked me not to change my mind.

When I did tell my mother, she burst into tears and kept on crying as if there had been a sudden death in the family. That was understandable. Audrey and I both expected that, as she told me in her letters. (I still have them).

I think it is important for the readers to get an idea of the extent of opposition that I faced to appreciate the "welcome" that Audrey could expect if I could get my parents to turn around. I kept her abreast of the turmoil our family was going through. At that time to get them to agree to my marrying a white Christian girl seemed practically impossible. Without their blessings Audrey's parents wouldn't support us and although we could get married without the blessings of both our parents, that would be starting off on the wrong foot. Neither Audrey nor I wanted to get married like that. At the same time I couldn't think of my not marrying her. As far as Audrey was concerned she was prepared to marry me without both our parents' blessings.

It was a status quo.

Although I joined the Company in their corporate office in Calcutta, my assignment was with their Explosives Factory—some 250 miles away in a place called Gomia in Bihar. I had to wait for a week or two for my housing to be ready. My stay in Calcutta gave me some time to discuss the proposition with my parents and my aunt (my mother's sister) and her husband. They were the only people who were in my camp! My four uncles and their wives were of the same opinion as my parents. My two younger sisters and their husbands gave me their tacit support but they didn't have much hope of my parents changing their minds.

I was in a quandary. I didn't know what else to tell my parents other than that Audrey *would* live with me as an Indian wife does for the rest of her life. But my parents couldn't envisage that and the fact remained that she was a Christian! We not only belonged to the Hindu faith but also were Brahmins, members of the highest caste.

I also let them know that she was not prepared to change

her religion. Strictly speaking, one can convert to Hinduism but most Hindus believe that you are born of Hindu parents and can't become a Hindu.

(I am digressing a little because it is unlikely that all Western readers will be aware of this issue).

I soon left Calcutta for my place of work. Our letters arrived in India and England almost on a daily basis! In the meantime Audrey's and my parents wrote to each other expressing serious doubt about the marriage to be a success. Audrey started writing to my father expressing how she looks at marriage and that she is fully aware of the hurdles a bi-racial marriage poses and how serious she was to make it a success. All of us were in great despair but neither Audrey nor I would change our minds. Audrey's letters helped my father to soften up a bit and finally condescended to bless us provided my mother did the same.

My probationary period in my job was one year. I would be confirmed if found suitable or would be let go if not after the first 12 months. I had no doubt about my confirmation— but only when confirmed that I would be eligible for leave. So I had to wait for at least one year before I could go over to England to marry Audrey provided I received my parents' blessings.

Audrey's parents wanted their only child to get married in their church to which I agreed, as I mentioned earlier.

The Director of the Company—a Scot called Jack Aitken— helped me in bringing our date of marriage forward. One day he asked me as to when I planned to get married. He obviously knew about my engagement. I said that I was waiting to complete my probationary period which I hoped to complete successfully. I had some nine months to go at that time. He asked me as to how soon I would like to get married. I said ASAP. He told me to go ahead to make the necessary arrangements. Even though I wouldn't have completed my probationary period, he said he would approve my leave on passionate ground!

I could have kissed him! Haven't heard a good news like that for a long time!

There was no E-mail those days and phone calls to England from Gomia (my place of work) in Bihar was difficult. I could only let Audrey know by post. So I wrote to her and went to see my parents the next weekend. I was pleased to see that their attitude had softened somewhat, and the fact that the Company Head was not only aware of Audrey but also encouraging me to hasten the process went in my favour.

My parents finally agreed!

I told them that we wouldn't let them down.

What then surprised me was that my Dad wanted me to have a full blown Hindu marriage which he wanted to organize!!

6 May 1961 was the date that Audrey's parents decided for our wedding. My parents agreed. This meant that I finally had their blessings. My mother's brothers and her only sister had a lot to do with changing my parents' minds. My aunt told my parents that they all had known me since my birth. A stay in England for three years didn't seem to have

changed their nephew, they said. She thought that the love was genuine and if my parents stuck to their guns, they doubted if I would change my mind. My fiancé, my aunt rightly thought, really did want to come to live in India as a member of our family and "we must trust them and welcome her as Anu's wife", she said. She also offered to give her away. Like the father gives her daughter away in an English marriage, a near relative, usually the father, does the same in a Hindu wedding.

While they changed their minds, my dad's brothers didn't. They told him that the marriage, although it was to be held according to the Hindu rites, with a Christian girl in the house (Hindu marriage in Bengal is held in the house) that belonged to all of them, would not be welcome as this would make the house "unholy". As it happened they had many daughters to be married off!!! This might pose a difficulty! (An anecdote about the Uncle who had the greatest objection appears later on which the readers might find interesting).

In deference to their wish, we had to find a different place for the wedding. Halls and houses are available for hire in Calcutta but there were no lists or websites (!) available in 1961, i.e. 52 years ago. One of my brothers-in-law was from Calcutta. It was a hard slog for him to find a suitable house, which he did. (I would be in his debt forever). It turned out to be a small palace in Calcutta which was available for hire by the then owner for weddings or parties.

It was 12 May 1961 when we were married—the fulfilment of my life's dream!

Looking back, there was this English girl who despite

serious opposition from her husband's family came to live for the rest of her life in a country she had never been to and knew very little about. She must have loved me very much indeed. I wonder what I would have done had the shoe been on the other foot.

My father gave a reception attended by some 300 guests which was customary for families of our standing in society. I doubt if there were many guests that evening who attended a wedding reception where the bride came from England!

We took the train the following evening for Gomia—an overnight journey from Calcutta. We got off the train at a station called Hazaribagh Road in the middle of the night, from where we were driven in a company car to Gomia. It was still dark when we arrived in our bungalow (a ranch style house).

No, I didn't carry Audrey into the house! The outside of the house was however decorated by one of my Bengali neighbours as is traditional for a wedding, which was a very pleasant surprise and a nice welcome for us, especially for Audrey.

We were still asleep (I think it was a Sunday) when we were woken by some six or eight Scottish ladies who had come to welcome Audrey. The company had its parent company in Scotland. Hence the wives of the senior staff were Scottish. Wasn't it nice of them! Later the Indian couple who decorated the outside of our house turned up to welcome her.

So our married life began. Before I left for England, I had

a man-Friday. He could only speak Hindi. With the lady of the house who didn't speak a word of Hindi, it took a while for both of them to communicate with each other in my absence other than by sign language!

We lived in Gomia for 9½ years. It would probably need an introduction for the reader to get an idea of the part of India Audrey found herself in.

'In the middle of nowhere' would be a fitting description! In the jungle of Bihar, an Eastern State of India, the company (Imperial Chemical Industries or ICI) started an Explosives Factory in the foothills of a mountain range. Indian Explosives Ltd (IEL) comprised 2000 acres of land including the housing community. The members of the management were provided with housing out of a total of some 1,200 employees. The benefits and the creature comforts went by the rank of the staff. Fortunately my management position made me eligible for a two-bedroom furnished house with one room air conditioned and the usual amenities. Audrey liked it and to be together by ourselves as man and wife—we were in the Seventh Heaven!!! (In fact we used to address each other in our letters when I was in India as "My Darling Husband" and "My Darling Wife" before we got married—very romantic)! I used to be thrilled to receive her letters addressed to "My Darling Husband"! Suppose she felt the same way receiving my letters.

The community in Gomia was very cosmopolitan. Apart from six or so Scots and their British wives, the rest of the senior staff came from all over India, most of them educated in the UK, Germany or the USA. Audrey therefore had no language problem as all Indian staff and their wives spoke very good English.

Right from the beginning she was very keen to learn Bengali. My conversation with her was rather stunted as I had to translate everything in Bengali at her request and wait for her to repeat after me perhaps more than once at times. I had to answer my own question to her in Bengali which she would then repeat after me!

I would be away at work for at least 10 hours a day for 5½ days a week.

Audrey found another teacher. Our next door neighbour had a little girl who after her KG class would come to our house to talk to Audrey in English and Bengali! Audrey used to have sweets for her which she was fond of. So the visits were quite regular. Later on we moved house when her teacher was Mrs. Chary from South India who spent many years in Calcutta and spoke fluent Bengali but with a South Indian accent. She was very gracious to spend considerable time with Audrey.

We never knew her first name as we in India traditionally addressed adults by their last names! Mrs. Chary was thrilled to have an English woman willing to learn Bengali from her. Audrey sucked in every Bengali word she learnt and practiced on me first thing when I would come back home from work. If I attempted to correct her accent of any word, in a defying voice, she would say, "How do you know? Mrs. Chary said that this word is pronounced like this! She speaks perfect Bengali!"

Life couldn't be better! We received the blessings of both our parents, although it involved writing numerous letters, coaxing, cajoling, and shedding blood and tears.

The community had a new resident from England and invitations poured in from my colleagues. She was somewhat unique as there was no Caucasian lady married to an Indian in the community, especially one who wore a sari and sindur (a red powder) on the parting of her hair (sign of a married woman) and tried to speak Bengali.

While it was a very welcome gesture on my colleagues' part, there was another side to it which didn't suit us at that time. It was the extra expenses for reciprocating the compliments. My net income (the Indian Income Tax rate was exorbitantly high) had to support my retired parents, which was customary in our society even if the parents didn't need financial assistance. I also had to support my brother's education and pay off my loan to Air India for my trip to England.

It wasn't very long before Baku, the gynaecologist wife of our Medical Officer Nari Ginwalla, announced the happy news! We were going to be parents! Everybody in India and England was overjoyed! My mother especially started praying for her first *grandson* instead of a granddaughter.

30th July 1962 saw the arrival of Neilamber—a healthy boy of over eight pounds—one year and three months after our wedding. There was a lot of discussion to choose his name. Even if the technology were available those days (which it wasn't) to find the gender in advance, we wouldn't have done it. So we had to think of names of boys and girls. It had to be an Indian name but one that could be shortened to an English name. My dad thought of many boys' names and no girls'! Nilamber, Niladri, Nilangshu are Bengali boys' names and each one could be shortened to Neil—an English boy's name. We chose Neilamber—another name for Lord Krishna.

The baby was born in Calcutta. The month of July in Calcutta is in the height of summer. We had to stay with my parents for a few days before it was medically safe for the baby to travel overnight by train. Fortunately Audrey and the baby could stand the heat (no Air Conditioner in my parents' house).

My mother came with us which was a tremendous help. It is customary for the mother of the new-born baby to engage a maid (called Ayah in Hindi). Audrey had told me that she would like to bring up her child herself. She was the only child of her parents and hence had not seen her mother bringing up a baby. I wondered how she would manage all that is required to handle a new-born baby. My mother sharing the work was a great help for Audrey. However my mother went back after a few months after which she was on her own. I was away at work from 7 to 12 and 2 to 5 or 6, sometimes even later. We had a help who could cook and help Audrey in other domestic jobs.

Compared to my siblings and cousins I saw when I lived in the extended family with my parents, Neilamber was a very good baby and hardly any trouble at all as I recall. He was the added attraction for my coming back home from work. I could see that Audrey was thrilled in her new role of mother. I still remember the music (not the lyrics) of some of the songs that she used to sing to lull him to sleep! I don't think I was that happy ever before. I could perhaps say the same for her. My parents would visit us quite often (being a retired Railway employee, he and my mother travelled free). We used to write to and hear back from my In-laws quite regularly.

The good life however was not to last long!

The performance of each management staff was assessed at the end of each year. I was called one day by the Factory Director Jack Aitken, the same man who helped to hasten our marriage. Jack told me that my performance was unsatisfactory and the company would like me to look for another job. In accordance with my terms of employment, employee or the employer had to give each other six months' notice of termination.
In my case the company would extend the notice period to twelve months, he said.

I had to find another job within the next twelve months. It was the worst news I had in my life. I was 30 then. The place of work was in the jungle of Bihar. Even the daily newspaper arrived on the third day. The type of job I would like to have was rarely advertised in the paper those days. I had the vision of the end of my life in India with my English wife, contrary to our plan of living in India for good.

I was terribly depressed, as were my parents and In-laws. Audrey was the only one who took it in her stride. "Try your best," she said, "If nothing comes up, there is life beyond ICI" (the name of the company). If we we had to go back to the UK, she could start working almost immediately and we could live with her parents to begin with.

With the limited availability of Employment Agencies and Newspaper Ads., the progress was very slow. However I managed to find a job in my field with the Indian Govt. in Hyderabad in the south with a salary cut of 30% .There would be hardly any chance of saving up for Audrey and Neil to visit England. That didn't bother her. I was very surprised and impressed by her positive attitude.

We have had problems of worse kinds during nearly 50 years of our married life. I have been depressed but she always had an optimistic attitude which helped us in tackling the problems.

I however didn't have to leave the company. With some six months left of my one-year notice period, the company transferred me from Research to Operations. The company had a plant making gunpowder and safety fuses. I had the job of a Shift Manager. Seven months later I was given the responsibility to co-ordinate the activities of four other Shift Managers and soon after I was promoted to be the Operations Manager reporting to the Plant Manager.

I never looked back from there.

One might wonder as to how from being at the bottom of the class I was suddenly the golden boy. The answer to that had nothing to do with my performance at work. It was all to do with what I (and my wife) did not do in our social life.

Audrey the English belle did not live the life of an English woman and her Indian husband encouraged her to do so. My British colleagues, especially my immediate boss, a Scot, disliked it and made it clear to me that we didn't drink, Audrey only wore saris, didn't dance and didn't snog with them at parties! She lived with her Indian husband as most Indian wives did. My Indian colleagues not only noticed that but were impressed by Audrey's genuine and successful efforts to integrate herself into the Indian way of life. So when I reported to an Indian boss in my new job, he was aware of the situation I was in and encouraged me to make it a success, which was in Operations, involving people who interested me and my performance was soon appreciated.

In the meantime we had wonderful news. Audrey was expecting our second child! We had a request from my in-laws that they would like one of their grandchildren to be born in England. We planned for Audrey to be with her parents well in advance of the arrival of the baby. It of course meant my living alone, but then I had a minimum of a 12-hour working day and my parents paid frequent visits.

One of my colleagues gave me a wonderful idea for which I would be in his debt forever. He suggested that I should ask Jack, the Factory Director, if it would be possible for me to visit the UK on business around the arrival time of the baby. I didn't think that he would entertain such a request.

I took my colleague's advice and was thrilled when Jack told me a few days later that he would like me to go to the Company's UK Factory in Ardeer, Scotland, to train for the position of Operations Manager of the Detonator Plant that was to be built there to substitute the imported product.

During the six weeks training there, I had enough funds left over from my generous expense account to be able to see Audrey, Neil and my In-laws in St Helens over the weekends. It worked out very well. Soon after I joined them, having completed my training, the baby arrived!! It was a beautiful girl of 9 pounds 10 oz with a headful of black hair! We had to have a name for her as we were to sail back to India in the next couple of weeks.

I don't know if it was possible those days in England to know the baby's gender in advance. We weren't interested in that, so we had thought of quite a few names of boys and girls—mostly boys' names from my father. There was a famous Bengali writer whose two daughters were called Sita and Shanta. I liked the name Shanta and thought to name our daughter, if we had one, by that name which Audrey also liked. My In-laws and parents also liked the name. I had to rush to get her Birth Certificate and have the name included in Audrey's Passport with hardly a few days left before the sailing.

It was a 3-week sailing from Liverpool to Bombay! Short of the kitchen sink we had everything to take back, not by choice but by mother-in-law's command!

Both of us hardly remember much about the sailing. Pretty uneventful. The 8-week-old baby and 2½ year old Neil must have been exceptionally good for us not to remember much except that Neil used to eat five ice creams a day and bit a girl whose parents were naturally not pleased!

Looking back, the voyage didn't seem so long. The boat stopped at Aden which was a shoppers' paradise then (it was February 1965). Audrey bought a small wooden camel with a flat leather seat which Neil and Shanta rode regularly and still couldn't break it. It is 48 years old now and still in fair condition in Shanta's house! All of her three sons must have had numerous rides on it too!

With our mountains of luggage, we could never clear the Customs had we not been met by a gentleman from the Bombay Office of my Company. I still remember the name—one Mr. Wilson. When he saw my luggage for which I had made a list, he asked me if I could spare 100 Rupees. (I didn't have to have it then and there). I agreed and surprise, surprise, everything went off very smoothly! Mr. Wilson took the luggage away in a van and we went in a separate company car to the hotel that had been booked by the company. It was on the seaside and was quite a good one.

Nearer the time of reaching Bombay, Audrey caught a bad cold while on the ship and lost her voice. She had to see a doctor in Bombay and fortunately she got her voice back by the time we reached Calcutta.

The train journey from Bombay to Calcutta took two nights. We had a 2-berthed air-conditioned compartment. I took the upper berth. Audrey shared the lower one with Neil. Shanta slept in her stroller. It had a hammock which was made like a baby bed. You lift the baby up and the hammock and the stand folded to a neat package—very handy.

The children must have been very good travellers, for, the next morning as I was standing in the corridor of the train, I met an Englishman who coincidentally was going to the same factory where I worked. He was very surprised when told that we were their (the man and his wife) next door neighbour and had our two kids with us. They never heard them! He said that they could never travel with their kids so quietly!

Practically the whole Sanyal and Bagchi (my mother's maiden name) clans turned up at the station—a real big reception committee! One of my Uncles said Shanta was a big bouquet of white flowers!

The travel back to our home in Gomia meant another overnight train journey. So after a few days with my parents, we travelled from Calcutta to Gomia. How we did that whole journey—sailing for three weeks, train travel for over 1200 miles and overnight train again—I don't know. Most surprisingly the kids did extremely well.

Our family now had another member. Audrey was used to bringing up Neil. But with Neil (2½) and Shanta (3 months) they were a handful. So we engaged a help—a middle-aged lady called Sushila. She and Shanta took to each other very well, which was a small mercy.

Life settled down to the usual routine. Shanta was an exceptionally quiet baby. Slept very well. Once she was missing (!) which gave us a real fright. She could sit up and crawl after a fashion. We had a large living room. Audrey had sat her down somewhere in one corner. Shanta could sit up by then obviously. She hardly made any sound let alone crying. Audrey got on with her household chores and after a while wanted to feed her. She looked for her everywhere, called her by her name (She couldn't respond though)—there was no Shanta! Audrey looked for her in every room, in case she had crawled away from the living room. After a considerably long search, she found Shanta exactly where she had sat her down! Shanta must have sat there for a good hour! Audrey had forgotten where she had sat her down! Shanta was true to her name, as Shanta in Bengali (or Sanskrit) is an adjective meaning feminine gender of quiet. Yes, Bengali adjectives have genders.

One aspect of our family life that stands out in both of

our memories is the stream of guests, unannounced in most cases. I suspect the main attraction was to see Anu's Bengali-speaking English wife in sari, cooking and serving Bengali food.

With her somewhat limited knowledge of Bengali then, she had a knack of making the guests feel at home. One particular episode stands out in our memory. One afternoon a car arrived unexpectedly. Out came one of my uncles (mother's brother) followed by seven other men and women! Yes! Eight people from one car! My Uncle's brother-in-law worked in the nearby Fertilizer factory. This man came along with his wife and two kids, his In-laws, my Uncle and Aunt—that made eight. We had a two-bedroom bungalow and a small living room. That had to house ten people plus our two babies for the night. Audrey had to cook for the extra eight people! She took these surprise visits in her stride. Can't say that we loved having these surprises too often but then it was a Bengali household we are talking about! In the 60s with practically no house telephones, these visits were not uncommon.

I am sure these surprise visits in India have gone now.

We lived literally in the middle of nowhere. We had one convenience store for basic ingredients like rice, etc., and a daily bazaar under the open sky for vegetables. The butcher would bring the goats and after they were slaughtered in the open, the meat would be bought by the waiting people. If you were late, the butcher's makeshift shop would be a piece of blood-stained ground!

Fishermen would call door-to-door with fresh fish and you better stock up because you might not see them for a week or longer. A man on a cycle would come with two pots of sweets hanging on each side of his handlebars. That is your only source of readymade desserts. Again you stock the sweets in case unannounced guests arrive at 10 at night! That did happen a few times during our stay there.

We made our own entertainment since Hazaribagh, the nearest town, was 30 miles and Ranchi 70 miles away. Ranchi is a city and later came to be the capital of a new State called Jharkhand. We went there for our shopping. One of my cousins lived there. Her husband was a physician. We were very well received and always stayed with them.

As regards our in-house entertainment, we had a weekly screening of movies in the Club House. In summer we sat outside and got eaten by mosquitoes! We also held dances. A Cultural Committee ran the entertainment. I served as its Secretary for two years. The Club House had all the usual amenities—bar (of course!), a swimming pool, rooms for billiards, table tennis, card games etc. and a library. Audrey was asked to look after it. She was pleased to do so and soon it was a well-stocked library.

Somebody suggested staging a play. As the Cultural Secretary it was my job to organize it. I have acted in school plays but have never directed any. Although the members of our community came from all over India and spoke different mother tongues, the common language of communication was English, not only in the Factory but also on social occasions. So it had to be an English play.

The members of the Senior Management were British. They were all in favour of the idea. We never had amateur dramatics there. The Managing Director of the Company sat in the Corporate Office in Calcutta. (The city has recently been named Kolkata, but during the 60s and 70s that we are referring to it was called Calcutta, the name which I have used throughout this book).

On hearing the news about the proposed play, the wife of the Burra Sahib (the Big Boss in Hindi!) sent me a few books. We decided to stage a comedy. The play we chose was called *Harlequinade* by Sir Terence Rattigan, a well-known English playwright of the 30s. It was about a touring theatrical family staging a production of Romeo and Juliet. The news caused quite an excitement in the community, especially amongst the ladies. Everybody wanted a part. Although I have forgotten all about the plot, Audrey remembered it as she told me many times. (She couldn't remind me again now from where she is!).

Every play has a limited number of characters and the people taking part have to have some empathy with the characters in the book. It caused a little problem for me. Although I was to direct and produce the play and it was my job to choose the cast, one member of the Senior Management (boss of my boss) expressed his displeasure to me as her wife was not offered a role in spite of her request. I never expected that there were so many people in the Jungle of India interested in the audition, i.e. there were more people wanting to take part than the number of roles! I forget the details but I think the Manager realized later that it was better that he didn't flex his muscles as it would not have gone in his favour since there were other ladies better than his wife for the particular role and there wasn't any other role that she could have. He didn't pursue it which was a great relief for me!

Audrey was one of the ladies wanting a role. I initially disagreed as I thought that the Indian audience wouldn't follow her accent. I finally condescended and in the event I was proved very wrong. The audience had no problem whatsoever following her. In fact she was by far the best actor. I didn't know her hidden talent!

The rehearsal started with great enthusiasm. Only I had two roles—that of the Director/Producer and the Chauffeur; as most members didn't have cars, I had to pick them up and take them back three or four times a week. Audrey also had several roles—rehearsing as well as cooking and serving snacks to the members of the cast. Neil, a little over one year old then, didn't like to be left alone. So to stop him from crying, Audrey had to carry him around while rehearsing!

We lived in Gomia for nearly ten years. Audrey, as she told me later on, liked the life in the middle of nowhere! We produced quite a few plays with Audrey in the cast as by then she had earned a reputation of being a good actor. I directed the plays, except in one case as the sole male member of the cast went down with flu, when with a couple of days' notice I had to take his role in addition to being the Director. I was a nervous wreck! Nevertheless it turned out to be a success.

Audrey also used to write, direct and produce Nativity plays where the employees' children took part. She was the Chief Cook and Bottle Washer.

We had an enjoyable social life in which Audrey took an active part like any other wife of the fellow employees.

She soon picked up Bengali—my mother tongue, the fourth most spoken language in the world. There were quite a few Bengali neighbours who soon became good friends. They were fluent in English but speaking to an English woman in Bengali was a novelty which brought us closer. One couple specially stands out—Arijit and Aruna Chakraverty. Even after I left the company in 1975 and lost touch, Aruna and Avirup (one of their two sons) tracked us down in 2002 and revived our friendship. Arijit by then had sadly passed away. Son Avirup, an Oxonian, and a prosperous Financial Consultant in London and Aruna are very kind to have kept in touch with us, especially after Audrey's sudden demise in 2010.

We probably would have stayed in Gomia for a few more years, but I asked for and received a transfer to another Division of the Company in Thane, a suburb of Bombay (now Mumbai), so that Neil could go to a good school. There was a residential school run by Missionaries in Hazaribagh, 30 miles away from Gomia. Neil didn't do well enough in the Admission Test. We were quite concerned as the Company's school in Gomia wasn't good.

In March 1970, we found ourselves in Thane, a District of the State of Maharashtra, 24 miles west of Bombay. We were housed in a Company's Apartment located on the Company's premises. It was a much smaller neighbourhood than Gomia.

After nearly ten years in the middle of nowhere, moving to a city close by the largest city of India was a very welcome change and a culture shock! We soon settled down. One could go to Bombay every day after office hours. In fact, members of a certain management level and above could spend a free weekend in a plush apartment in Hill Park, an exclusive area of Bombay. It had a resident cook who would cook any food you wanted. We used to look forward to our turn. There are so many things to do and see in Bombay.

Like Gomia, we had our Club House with all the entertainment facilities. Our in-house talents used to put up plays with me as the Director for my sins, Christmas Festivities, Bingo, monthly dances with live band etc. A good social life.

Even though we were some 1200 miles from Calcutta, my home, there was no dearth of visitors! Audrey, a Lancastrian (people of Lancashire, a county in the North West of England, are well known for their hospitality) lived up to her county's reputation!

There was a milestone in our life during our stay in Thane. Audrey's parents came to visit us and stayed for some three months. My parents also came to meet them and we all stayed in our Apartment. East and West met!!

Overlooking our Apartment was a small lake formed during the construction of the Factory. There was a sidewalk (footpath in England). Both our parents—Audrey's father in trousers and half-sleeve shirt, her mother in her frock, my mother in a sari and my father in Dhoti (a 5½ yard long white piece of cloth) and Punjabi (a loose shirt without collar) used to go out for a walk on most evenings round the lake. It was an unusual sight (we have a picture of them in this book) and most neighbours used to come out just to see the four elderly persons walking and chatting—people of different race and colour bonded together with love that started with their children.

That was perhaps one of the happiest periods of my life, a dream come true!

All good things must come to an end. Unfortunately nearer the end of their holiday with us, my father-in-law fell ill. He was fortunately well enough to catch their chartered flight but a week later we received a telegram to say that he had passed away! Pulmonary embolism—blood clot in the leg that climbs up to the lung and cuts off the oxygen supply to the heart; the same that Audrey died of.

Audrey could not fly out before three days after we got the news, as she had to renew her passport and there was a public holiday when the British High Commission was closed. As a result she missed the funeral.

I had suggested that Audrey (their only child) should stay with her mother for as long as she felt necessary before her mother had settled down. My parents fortunately were still with us. So they stayed back to look after Neil (9½) & Shanta (7).

I think in everybody's life Murphy's Law comes into play some time or other. A year earlier, one of my parotid glands (located near the jaws and produce saliva) got infected and needed a small operation. The same gland got infected again and swelled to a level which needed emergency surgery which ran the risk of damaging local nerves causing partial paralysis of a portion of the face.

I sent Audrey a telegram with the news and asked her to come back. By the time she arrived, the surgery was over with no side effect; but I had to stay in the hospital for a week. Our apartment in Thane was 25 miles from the hospital. Fortunately we had met one of my distant cousins in Bombay who had an apartment literally across the hospital. This was a Godsend. They invited the Sanyal clan to stay with them during my stay in the hospital.

It took months for the wound to heal. I had to carry on working with an enormous bandage on my right cheek. It finally left a beauty spot!

Neil stayed in the same hospital after his eye surgery to treat his squint. Only in this case it was pre-arranged. But Audrey had to stay with him as they bandaged both his eyes for a while.

So our life in India went along not quite on an even keel.

1973 was perhaps the worst year for our whole family until then, when one of my brothers-in-law in Kanpur, an industrial city of North India, didn't survive his second heart attack. I rushed from Thane—some 750 miles. Arriving by train, I was too late for the funeral. He was 43 and left behind my sister of 33 and three children—one girl (16), two boys (14 and 2).

He had a good job but didn't save. The Indian Govt. does not have any widow's pension or support. He stayed in a rented house. His life insurance policies were not renewed. His bank balance was tiny. His only asset, if you can call it that, was a rented apartment in Calcutta. The rent was overdue by several months! My brother and I paid up so that my sister and her children could stay there. India has an IRA (Individual Retirement Account) type scheme of the

USA called Provident Fund (PF). The amount in his PF was hardly anything to live on. We put that sum in a Fixed Deposit account accruing a meagre interest. Practically she and her family were entirely dependent on me and my brother who as an Engineer earned enough for his own family but was not in a position to provide substantial help. Even then he undertook the boarding and tuition fees for our eldest nephew. The main thrust fell on me. After meeting our own family expenses, supporting my retired parents and paying our son's boarding and tuition, the left over from my take home pay was not enough to support my sister to have even a subsistence level of living.

Audrey was all the way behind me and went through a fair amount of hardship. One anecdote of 1974 comes to my mind. She had bought a frock for Shanta for 20 Rupees (about 400 Rupees or around 5 Pounds in today's money). I asked Audrey if it was really necessary. Perhaps my tone of voice was of a higher decibel than normal. She started crying and said that she didn't mind wearing torn saris but she won't let her daughter wear torn frocks.

After meeting our commitments, we were lucky to have 100 Rupees left over in the Bank at the end of the month. We practically had no savings. I knew that I must support my sister with more money; only I did not know how to find the additional funds. For Audrey to get a job was not possible as we lived out of the city and her teaching diploma from Sheffield University was not regarded to be on a par with the equivalent Indian degree, assuming there were jobs available!

We went through quite a few sleepless nights. I scoured through the daily Newspaper Ads without success. Having lived out of the city area didn't help developing contacts. The money that had accumulated in my Provident Fund was not available to borrow from except if I left the country when the entire amount was available. If I put that sum in a fixed deposit scheme, the monthly interest would have been just enough for my sister to make both ends meet. I discussed the idea with Audrey and my parents. Audrey left it to me and did not want to take part in the decision making lest in future my family members would think that I went back to England because of my English wife. My parents and I agreed that there was no other alternative. That meant my leaving the country for good which was contrary to what Audrey and I decided before we got married. We wanted to live in India for good.

I was 40, having worked for nearly 15 years reaching a middle management position; the children were settled in schools, and Audrey had integrated herself into the society. Starting all over again in a Western country for a middle aged non-Caucasian was not easy.

I had to find a job first. The only foreign country I knew was Britain. I didn't fancy going back there as my memory as a student with respect to racial discrimination in the UK was not brilliant.

As a student there I had made two friends—Alan Hedley, one of my colleagues in my Department where I did my research, and Eric Priestley, a local successful businessman who was interested in projecting a favourable image of Britain to the foreign students. He regarded me almost as a member of his family and I held him in high regard. Alan stayed back in the Department as a lecturer after his Ph.D. I kept in touch with both of them through Christmas letters.

I asked Alan and Eric if they could get me some contacts as I wanted to come back to England. After a few reminders from me and Eric, I received a letter from Babcock & Wilcox (B & W), London, a household name in Boiler Engineering, that they had heard about me from Alan and they would be interested in the possibility of employing me in London.

B & W had a big presence in India. The Indian CEO at the request of B & W's London Office saw me in Bombay and a few days later I received a letter of appointment as a Design Engineer in their London Office. I received the offer with mixed feelings. The interest from my savings fund would make it possible for my sister to have a subsistence level of living and her children would go to school and college. In return I had to leave my country as well as a very good management job and start at entry level at the age of 40 in a Mechanical Engineering field completely unfamiliar to me. In India I was an Operations Manager in a Chemical Company of International reputation.

I accepted the offer after discussing my situation with my parents. There was no other way for me to provide the financial assistance for my sister and her family to have a subsistence level of living.

Audrey declined to take part in the decision making as she strongly felt that her consent might be construed as an excuse for her to leave India to return to her country. She repeatedly told me that it has to be my decision and my decision only.

Audrey and the children left India late March 1975. They lived with her mother in her hometown St Helens and started teaching from the first Monday after their arrival!

The children joined the school Audrey taught at.

She had lived in India for nearly 14 years. She left the country contrary to our plan. I wondered as to what her overall impression of India was. I had asked her numerous times to write her autobiography which she started but stopped after writing about her early days.

Her interest changed to genealogy where she developed a Family Tree of 1001 names mostly comprised of her parents' ancestors. It included only a few of *my* direct relations and ancestors despite her repeated requests. I never got round to finding out any other ancestors mainly because of laziness. The absence of a system of keeping records of birth, marriage and death in India during those days didn't help. She soon stopped bugging me.

Her interest changed to writing historical novels and she intended to write a trilogy. She published two—*Talavera* and *Naseby*. She passed away just after starting her last one.

In fact the phone call (last one of her life) that she took from her school friend Norma Smyth (little over an hour before she drew her last breath) was about her book. I overheard Audrey telling Norma that she had the plot and all the characters mapped out! In fact she did write a few lines.

There will never be a trilogy by Audrey Sanyal!
Whenever I brought up the topic of resuming writing her autobiography, she always told me she didn't like writing about people who were alive. When I reminded her after my parents had passed on, she didn't like to dwell on the subject and said that she would go back to her autobiography after she had completed her trilogy. Somehow she never got

around to putting pen to paper about her days in India. I can only guess her thoughts. She liked my people—parents, siblings and my 19 cousins and their families in general, but did not want to put down her impressions of some of the things which in her opinion I can only presume were not that complimentary.

She was totally integrated into a middle class Bengali society of the 60s/70s. She picked up Bengali within about two years after she had lived in India and was soon fluent. We mostly spoke Bengali to each other including her last talk to me in 2010! She wore a sari, cooked Bengali dishes, and observed Bengali customs.

One anecdote I recall that Rupa, my sister-in law, told me. A custom that most mothers in Bengal observe is to fast (no water even) from dawn to dusk for a day and pray to *Sashti* (Goddess of children) for the well-being of their children. Audrey decided to fast with my sister-in-law who was visiting us on one such occasion. That day the temperature was over 40 C/104 F (no air-conditioner) and in the late afternoon both were parched and famished. My sister-in-law asked Audrey to have a drink of water. Audrey told her that "your brother-in-law (she will not address me by my first name in keeping with the tradition of our family) told me that fast means not only no food but also no water!".

Another anecdote which must be mentioned is Audrey following my mother's tradition of touching my father's feet every day with her right hand when he went to work and putting her hand on her head. This symbolizes showing the respect the wife has for her husband by taking the dust off his feet and putting it on her head. This in our society is done or used to be done during the 50s/60s also by any man

169

or woman to show respect for his/her elders. We also used to do that to our parents and our elders and still do it.

Audrey used to do that every day when I went to work and carried on most of her life; only later on, she used to do it whenever I was going away for a while.

One morning when we were in India and I was going out to work, she asked me to wait for Neil—a toddler then. When he joined me Audrey was using a sign language which was completely unknown to me. I said, "What's going on?" Audrey then said to Neil, "Do what I told you to do." I found the toddler bending down and trying to touch one of my feet. I then realized what he was up to! I picked him up and kissed him. It was a day I always remember!

Audrey never ceased to amaze me. Her sincerity in observing our family customs and traditions throughout her life was truly astonishing, even though she left India in 1975 and lived there for 14 years. She went back a few times for short periods after that.

Her last visit was in 2004 to attend my nephew's wedding.

She cared for my relatives as if they were her own. One instance sticks out in my memory. Long after we came back to England, emigrated to the US and re-bought a house in England, we always kept in close touch with my family in India. One day when one of my nephews (son of my sister for whom I left India), had called us, I enquired about the weather in Calcutta. It happened to be the monsoon season. He told me that their bedroom of their rented apartment leaked like sieve and most nights he and his wife had to put a tarpaulin on the bed, move to the spare single bedroom and spend practically sleepless nights. (The landlord won't do any repair work as there was a lawsuit on and he would love my nephew to leave). While this conversation was going on the speakerphone so that Audrey could hear and take part, she suddenly interrupted and asked me to ask him how much an apartment of their size would cost in a good area of Calcutta. I converted the cost in Rupees that my nephew told me into Pound Sterling and gave her the figure. Split seconds later Audrey asked me to tell him to look for such an apartment! My nephew and his wife who were listening to the conversation started crying and her decision surprised me as the idea of buying them an apartment never crossed my mind. They spoke to Audrey at great length expressing their gratitude. I had Audrey's strict instructions not to share this information with any of my relatives including my only brother!

They shortly moved into their new abode and had no further use of a tarpaulin!

I was indeed blessed!

*   *   *

England here I come!

I arrived in London some ten days after they arrived and started working from 1 April 1975 for the new company Babcock & Wilcox in South London.

Audrey carried on teaching in St Helens.

After my statutory probationary period was over when I could expect to keep working for them for the time being, we decided that she would try looking for a job in London. It didn't take her long to find one. Her stay in India and skill in speaking Bengali and understanding Hindi helped her in getting the position of Head of an ESL (English as a Second Language) Centre in North London. I was staying in digs (a colloquial word for lodging in somebody's house) in North London. We decided to leave the children in St Helens with my mother-in-law until we could rent a house. Renting a house in London was and still is not cheap.

Knowing it would hardly be possible, I asked Audrey if the Council of Barnet (where the school was located) would have any housing facility for their staff as I was provided with Bungalows (an English word for a ranch style house) and Apartments by my ex-employer in India. She asked her boss and was told that housing was available for key members of the Council. He recommended that she should apply for categorization of her position. Low and behold she was told that her job *was* in the key member category as teaching English (especially as Head of the Centre) to non-English children was a Specialist teaching function. When she saw the Director of Housing of the Council, she was shown a map of North London and asked where she would like to live as *three* houses were available nearby her school! She obviously chose the nearest one—one and a half minutes' walk on the same footpath (sidewalk) at a weekly rent of some nine pounds (approximately $15) which is about 100 pounds ($160) in 2012 Pound Sterling.

We were over the moon!

In the next eighteen months, we saved enough (we arrived

172

in the UK with empty pocket as the Indian Govt. didn't allow any Rupee exchange those days) to put a deposit down for our first house—a semi-detached (duplex) 3-bedroom house in Colindale in North London—a respectable residential area, within walking distance from the Colindale Underground station and one stop for Audrey's school and some 40 minutes to my South London Office.

We had our children transferred from St Helens and got them admitted to local London schools.

Audrey and I enjoyed our work; the children were settled in their school. Audrey's mum in St Helens and my mother and the rest of my family in India were all well.

Life was once again on an even keel.

We went on holidays in England as well as India and shortly bought a bigger house in the same area. My work responsibility went up which involved frequent travelling both in the UK and overseas. I was away sometimes for weeks (longest being six weeks at a stretch) when Audrey had to look after the household on her own.

The reason behind moving to a bigger house was not only to be able to spread ourselves a bit, but mainly for my widow mother-in-law to stay with us. She felt lonely in her big house in St Helens and wanted to move in with us. We welcomed the idea. Her stay turned out to be short lived. She felt that she had lost her independence although she had her own living and bedrooms but not her own kitchen. She didn't think that we spent enough time with her and she missed her church and friends. A few months after she moved in she went back to her own house. We were very sorry to see her go. We used to visit her as often as possible. She passed away due to a heart related problem within a year.

The children completed their school-leaving exam., called GCSE (General Certificate of Secondary Education) "O" (Ordinary) level which one takes at the age of 16, that being the mandatory school-leaving age in the UK. Depending on the grade one achieves, the school allows the student to read for another two years for GCSE A (Advanced) level, after which one can go to University.

Education from primary school to Degree level was free those days (70/80s). In addition students from financially disadvantaged families received Govt. grants depending on their parents' income. This changed later. While education up to high school is still free, university education is not; students can and do take bank loans refundable over a period afterwards depending on the income of the graduate.

Both our children did well and went to University. When son Neil graduated with an Honours degree in Chemistry from London University, the country was in severe economic depression and jobs were scarce. He went for further education in Information Technology to find work. When our younger child Shanta graduated, the job situation had improved and with her Honours degree in Business Studies, she found work quite quickly in Coventry where they lived.

While still at the University, she got married to Davinder (a Sikh), a University friend of son Neil, and soon presented us with our first grandson.

Audrey and I were ecstatic! It was one of the best news in our life. Our friends who were grandparents had told us that you will never appreciate the feeling unless you become one.

We called him Arjun—the name of the 5th Sikh Guru and also one of the Pandhava brothers in *Mahabharata* the famous Hindu epic. The teachings of Lord Krishna to Arjun comprise *Bhagabatgita,* the Hindu equivalent of the Bible.

Shanta was still at the University. She was sponsored by my Employer in London which required her to work for the sponsor during her summer breaks. She and Arjun stayed with us then. He grew up to be an exceptional person perhaps in all senses of the word, but he was certainly an exceptional baby with regard to his sleeping habit. He didn't sleep at night and slept during the day! He would wake up countless number of times at night. His mother slept in another room. So the grandma, a schoolteacher, who was on her summer holidays, slept with the baby.

I have never seen my wife in such a bad mood throughout that period as she had to wake up every time the baby woke up. She however couldn't sleep all day as she had to do all the household chores.

During our time in London, I was very pleased to have my widow mother visit us twice. The first time she came, we had no problem with bedrooms but only had a tiny kitchen. She was a strictly vegetarian orthodox Hindu widow. As we are non-vegetarian, she cooked her own food after "cleaning" the kitchen worktop with water containing some from the Holy River Ganges (which she brought from India) which also had little cow dung (yes, you read that right!) which she also brought with her! Both are sacred to Hindus, especially for the orthodox ones. Audrey did her shopping which she placed on top of the piano in the living room instead of in the fridge. She brought her own milk bottle the Milkman put outside the front door of the house. We, including me, were not allowed to touch the bottles! The fact that the milk was supplied by a Christian Milkman did not matter! Her shopping was also not done by a Hindu!

My mother was not very consistent in her orthodox practices, not just in England but as long as I had known her.

Next and the last time she visited us in England, she had a living room of her own where we put a Hot Plate. She was very pleased—no kitchen top cleaning was required with cow dung anointed Ganges water!

We were very fortunate that she did manage to come to London for the second time. She saw Arjun—her great grandson. Arjun remembers her although he was probably 3 at the time.

Audrey had a high level of respect for and interest in other religions and practices. She obtained a better teaching position in South London than she had in North London. The job involved teaching the children, mostly of the Christian faith, about other religions, their customs and ceremonies. Her classroom was full of pictures of Hindu Gods and Goddesses, Buddha, traditional clothes of members of different religions. For example during *Dewali*, the main Hindu religious festival, she used to organize short plays on themes from Hindu Epics—*Ramayana* or *Mahabharata*—where the children in traditional clothes took part. Once she had to handle an emergency—the child playing *Lakshmana,* brother of King *Rama,* fell ill shortly before the play and she had to find a substitute.

Her contribution was well recognized by the School Management.

Audrey was not lucky on the health front in later years. When she started her new job in South London, we were still in North London despite our best efforts to move before she started. One prospective seller changed his mind the night before the contract was to be signed. So to go to her new school, she had to take the London Underground—27 stops each way, from almost one end (Colindale) of the Northern Line to the other. Audrey firmly believed that this stress of travelling started her Irritable Bowel Syndrome (IBS)—a widespread condition involving recurrent severe abdominal pain and diarrhoea or constipation, often associated with stress, depression—and Diverticulitis (**pouches or diverticula that form in the wall of the colon causing severe pain**). These ailments stayed with her for the rest of her life and finally were instrumental for her demise.

We lived in London from 1975 to 1991 before moving to America. Out of these 16 years she suffered from frequent attacks of IBS which made her very ill at times. She saw the best consultants that our Primary Care Physicians recommended. After numerous consultations she was finally told that IBS is incurable but not fatal. She accepted it and taught herself to live with it. She didn't find it easy. She would have bouts of IBS with no rhyme or reason and unrelated to her diet. She would have to take to bed at a moment's notice. Sometimes it would take her up to a week to get back to normal! If that is not enough, she was often down with flu. It put a lot of restraint on our extra-curricular activities. We hardly went out to eat. She was reticent about eating in a restaurant. She was also reluctant about booking any holiday as she feared that she might be down with IBS. (She had the last major operation after we had booked a holiday).

When Audrey started having frequent bouts of IBS and was bedridden, the children were grown up and could look after themselves.

It depressed me very much as there was nothing I could do.

Despite her chronic illness, she managed to lead as normal a life as she could. She worked full-time as a teacher and had to go through her household chores. It wasn't easy.

I asked her one day about her stomach pain. She told me that she had stomach pain practically all the waking moments of the day. She would let me know the day she didn't have any pain.

How much pain she must have had to endure! Very rarely would she complain about her pain to me. On one occasion when we were living in Florida, she was taking me to Orlando airport—a drive of an hour and a half. Hardly an hour or so before we were starting out, her IBS pain began. There was no taxi service available at such short notice where we lived. There was no time to ask a neighbour. I will never forget the fact that with such intense stomach pain, she took me to the airport and came back.

British stiff upper lip and undying love!

We lived in London for 16 years in four houses. The steady flow of visitors as we used to have (mostly self-invited) from India and the USA continued unabated! Audrey had to look after them which was less of a burden if they came during her school holidays, but they came when it suited them. She not only cooked extra food for the visitors but also prepared sandwiches for them when one particular family (who we didn't know that well) of four went out for sight-seeing in the late afternoon and bemoaned the fact that the places were mostly closed! Audrey thought that her sandwiches would save them some money. I told her that our visitors were already saving hundreds of pounds in hotel money and could well afford some lunch, but she nevertheless carried on with her sandwiches!

She had her inherent quality of Lancastrian hospitality. Once while I was flying from London to Bombay, I sat next to two German physicians who were on their holiday to India. They hadn't booked any hotels. When I got home and told her about them, she told me that I should have invited them to come and stay with us!

Once we had some visitors when we were away on our holiday (they changed their date which clashed with our pre-booked holiday). On that occasion our son Neil looked after them.

I used to visit America at least twice a year on business. In 1990 I ran into a business friend of mine, an Executive Vice President of a reputable Consulting Engineering Research Company. He told me they were looking for somebody to oversee some major Projects and asked me if I would like to help them. The work interested me. I had another job offer then from a global Consulting Engineering Company in Chicago. He offered me higher compensation and agreed to my terms and conditions.

I had reached the highest position that I could in the London Company and could not go up any further in my career progression. I had quite a few years left before I retired. Leaving England meant that Audrey had to leave her teaching position. She had reached a senior grade, happy with her job and being in America, we wouldn't see our family and especially grandson as often.

Audrey however was quite happy to leave her job. She felt she had enough of teaching and as her health was not so good, she didn't mind finishing with teaching although she had not reached her retiring age. An Insurance company bought her pension contribution from her Employer and she started getting pension from the Insurance Company and also received a lump sum amount.

I left my company in June 1991 and joined the US company located in Orrville, Ohio—a tiny city (population 8,000) 50 miles south of Cleveland, Ohio. Her school asked her to complete the academic year to which she agreed. She came over during the summer holiday when we bought a house in Orrville. She went back to complete the school year and joined me in January 1992.

For both of us it was a massive change. I won't be surprised if more than 8,000 people lived on the Road (in Wimbledon area of South London) where we had our house!

Other than my supervisor, Todd Sommer, whom I had met before moving in from London, we didn't know anybody in Orrville. Audrey to begin with was busy setting up the household. I had a friend in Cleveland from my Indian University days. Dr Ron Datta, his nephew Asim and his wife Sunanda were of immense help to us. We also had somewhere to go during the weekend.

Orrville was a picture postcard place! One Traffic Light, one supermarket and two banks! No public transport, no taxi service. Very green and leafy! Our house was on the top of a small hill with a wood at the back. It was a retreat rather than a house. We loved it. She got her first car and she used to drive around exploring the countryside. (In England we had two cars and at one time three, but she couldn't drive as she failed her Driving Test twice and our children and I couldn't get her back to the Driving School!).

We soon got to know quite a few locals through the church and the Rotary Club. The Realtor who found the house for us introduced Audrey to the Ladies Book Club and Garden Club. She and for that matter I were "novelties", as we were the only English and Indian residents of the city. Whenever we went shopping or to the Bank or any such place, she soon had a small crowd around her! People just wanted to listen to her English accent! Very few of the locals have been to England or have met English people. We quite enjoyed the fame while it lasted! We soon were invited to speak at Churches or at the Rotary Club. I received a princely sum of $5(!) from The Book Club for my talk about my travel to Singapore.

Having to go to teach in London even when she suffered from IBS or flu put her under considerable stress. Not having to go to school in Orrville was a sheer release! I could see how happy she was. When I would ask her, which I did quite often, as to what she felt when she woke up every morning, her reply every time was that it was sheer joy as she wouldn't have to go to school ever again. When I would ask her in jest if she would like to take up a part-time job, she would reply, "Only if you want to force me to go back to work!" 16 years of teaching was enough for her, she said.

She used to say she never felt bored and enjoyed doing nothing!

We lived in Orrville, Ohio, for a little over three years before we moved to Oakbrook Terrace, a suburb of Chicago, Illinois.

There were quite a few milestones in our life during this short period in Ohio. On the positive side, our second grandson Amar (now 21!) was born. I started my consultancy business (100 x $1 shares, Audrey and I owning 50 shares each). It was a risk in our Accountant's opinion. In his experience this type of one-man band type business does not last long. That was in 1994; in 2013 as I write this it is still bringing in revenue! I suppose we were fortunate. The business turned out to be a wise decision both financially and from the point of view of job satisfaction.

Our children, friends and relatives from England and India visited us in Ohio. During this period, I lost my younger sister in India due to a serious stroke. Audrey had two surgeries both in England—for haemorrhoid and hysterectomy. She recovered from both without any hitch. I had to be in America during her first operation. Fortunately our son Nilamber (Neil) was then working from our home in London which was a big help.

My business required me to move to Chicago. Audrey was recovering in London. I had to move by myself; our Ohio friends were very helpful.

She left Ohio for England for the operations but came back to Chicago as I had moved there by then. Her trip was from London to Toronto; from there to Cleveland and on to Chicago. There was a surprise reception committee of our friends for her at Cleveland airport! Neither of us knew about it. Audrey was very, very pleased.

I had rented an apartment in Oakbrook Terrace and made some friends. Dr Subrata Banerjeee and his wife Bakul, also a doctor, were particularly close. He drove me to Midway airport to meet Audrey and asked us to stay with them (although both of them were working) so that they could look after us until she was well enough to go back to our place.

Audrey and I will be in their debt forever!

It was not long before she got her strength back. She was not allowed to lift even 5 lbs (around 2.5 Kg) to begin with.

She was an indispensible help to the business. It involved my visiting Clients and reporting my findings. The reports could be quite long at times and their delivery was always time constrained. To save time I used to tape the reports and my longsuffering wife used to transcribe them. As the business picked up so did the report writing frequency. I asked my Accountant if I could make her an employee and pay her for her efforts. The Accountant advised against it as it involved not just the salary but also other payments like matching her contribution towards her retirement etc. Thus she went on putting in long hours at times without any compensation.

All for love!

She had to type a long report at a very short notice before we were due to come back to England for the summer in 2010. That was her last contribution to our business as she did not return to the USA. She passed away in the country she was born in!

As I mentioned earlier, my consultancy business picked up fairly quickly. We had been living in a rented apartment. We decided to buy a house as we found we could afford a single family home (American for a detached house). We moved to a house in Lisle, a small city, west of Chicago. There is a nearby railway station (Villa Park) to the city. I had to go to one of my clients' office in Chicago downtown area three days a week. The house was quite convenient. Audrey would drop and pick me up from the Railway station, as the parking area in those stations is not only small but pre-rented on a monthly basis.

The house was located in a picturesque woody area with a footpath at the back of the house leading to a pretty lake. By then the number of my clients has been rising and as a matter of coincidence the day we moved in our house in Lisle, I had to leave for Tokyo for a week, leaving Audrey to do all the unpacking and by the time I came back, I came back to a home (not a house). She had a knack of settling down in a new environment very quickly. Our Lisle house was our eighth (!) house including the houses in India and England.

One of the milestones of our family while we were in Lisle was our son's moving to Chicago from London. He was offered a position in an IT company in a Chicago suburb. We now had one child near us.

Before moving to Chicago, Neil had met Shomita (soon to be our daughter-in-law) from Chicago. One or the other was crossing the Atlantic every month. We were delighted when they announced their engagement. He moved to Shomita's apartment on the 47th Floor of a skyscraper called Water Plaza in downtown Chicago. It had a spectacular view especially in the evening. It felt as if you were in a plane and landing in a city!

When they announced their wedding plans, we decided to move to a bigger house. We rightly thought that we would have visitors for the wedding from India and England. (We did have nine guests staying with us). The same Realtor who found our house in Lisle helped us in finding a house in Naperville, the third largest city in Illinois.

It was a good move. Since moving to the US, I wanted to live in a big house which is quite common with middle class Americans; British people find it difficult to afford it even if you could find one. (My daughter's and eldest grandson's houses in England are exceptions).

Guests for wedding especially coming from India do not arrive the day before the wedding, nor do they leave straight after the event. It is customary for them to come well in advance and leave well after the event. In India, one usually has home helps and one could get additional temporary helps. This does not apply in the West. While I was getting additional supplies of food, Audrey was busy providing three meals a day for the guests. It was summer and although the houses are centrally air-conditioned, Audrey was busy practically from dawn to late night mostly cooking and serving. This was considered to be the normal standard of hospitality the guests expected. Having lived in India long enough, she was used to this, but this didn't help her health and she suffered from bouts of IBS during the stay of the guests. She did whatever had to be done regardless.

It would perhaps help Western readers to know the difference between Christian and Hindu weddings particularly from my part (West Bengal) of India. In a Christian wedding the groom's parents and their close relatives and friends are invited to the wedding and post-wedding receptions by the bride's parents. In a Hindu wedding, the groom's parents also hold a reception for relatives and friends. Audrey and I held a reception in our house. We catered the food as Indian caterers are available in Chicago since there is a large Indian Community. It was a very joyous occasion. My sister-in-law Rupa who came from India for the wedding with my brother Santimoy was most helpful. Audrey would have found it difficult to do it all by herself.

Also, a Bengali wedding involves many rites about which Audrey, a Lancashire girl, hadn't the foggiest idea! Rupa my sister-in-law advised her on these and Audrey observed every single one! She need not have bothered, but she had great respect for Bengali traditions. She never ceased to amaze me, knowing how seriously she took them, which could only come from her deep love for me!

Shomita—our Bengalee daughter-in-law's parents live in

Stamford, Connecticut. The wedding took place in a 5-Star hotel there. It was a Bengali wedding in every detail. Chitra, her mother, was very particular about observing the wedding rites, which impressed me very much considering she spent most of her adult life with her parents in Pakistan, and was educated in England & France.

The whole event went off very smoothly and the guests left (Audrey and I were making regulars trips to Chicago O'Hare airport at one time) and we could do with a holiday (vacation in American)!

Now we had our son and daughter-in-law nearby in downtown Chicago—an hour's drive from Naperville. So we saw them often and went out together.

*   *   *

Life however never runs smoothly.

Uncertainty is the only thing that is certain in life!

While I was enjoying my work travelling within the country and Overseas, I started having momentary pain in the centre of my chest which would go away in a matter of a few seconds. But those few seconds felt like a long time. When I saw my Primary Care Physician (GP in England), he immediately had my ECG done. He was perfectly happy with the result, he said. He put it down to muscular pain and prescribed some medicine for that. However, the pain kept on coming and wasn't related to anything and could occur any time of the day or night. My return visit to the doctor led to a referral to a Cardiologist. My ECG while on treadmill (aka Stress Test) and ultrasound were satisfactory. My doctor showed me the Specialist's report. While both were happy, the intermittent pain did not stop. My doctor at my request sent me for a second opinion. This Cardiologist was also happy with the report but suggested that there is a gold standard called Angiogram which would show details of the heart and its functioning. He didn't expect any surprise and "guaranteed" (this is the exact word he used) that my heart was OK. When he came back to the room where I was lying down after the procedure, he was preceded by Audrey. One look at her and I could tell something was not right. The same doctor—Dr Jaid—told me that I am a lucky man and while I expected to hear that the result only confirmed his prediction, he said there was a severe blockage in one of the main arteries. In response to my question as to what the next step would be, he said that I had to be operated upon the next morning!!! It would be open heart surgery in the nearby hospital to which I was rushed in the next few minutes in an ambulance so that I could be admitted the same evening!

From a perfectly normal human being, I became a patient awaiting open heart surgery in a matter of a couple of hours!

Fortunately our son Neil worked in the city of Chicago. Audrey knew the name of the company but not his office phone number. The hospital tracked him down.

Audrey and Neil informed our daughter in England and my brother and other close relatives in Calcutta before the surgery.

It took seven hours, involving bypassing four blocked arteries instead of one!

I came home after four nights in the hospital.

While I thought I had a 50:50 chance of success, I accepted the possibility of that day being the last day of my life.

Audrey told me that that thought never crossed her mind.

She was an introvert, a quiet person. I am the exact opposite. But when necessary she could rise to the occasion and was an excellent conversationalist. She also had a very strong strength of mind. The fact that she, the only child of her parents, left them and her country to join her husband to live permanently in a completely unknown country bears testimony to her willpower.

This unwarranted heart surgery not only changed my lifestyle but also was a constant worry for Audrey, especially when my post-surgery chest soreness turned out to be incurable arthritis which sapped my energy. Audrey did not let me do household work involving lifting any weight for the rest of her life. She also used to tell me that she didn't worry half as much for her IBS as she did for my heart. For years she kept a suitcase ready with my overnight clothes etc., in the event of an emergency visit to the hospital.

An emergency trip to hospital has not been necessary for me as I write but it was necessary for her and she never came back from her second emergency visit!!

This surgery had a significant effect on my professional life. Being short of physical energy, I found it difficult to take up more work and undertake travelling. I had to visit one of my clients three days a week. That started becoming more and more difficult. I also had hypoglycaemia which added to my misery. Audrey suggested I leave that work and retire as I did not have to work. I took her advice.

We also decided to downsize as the house was too big for the two of us and we also wanted to pay off our mortgage. We did not want to leave the area having lived there for some eight years. She however did not like the houses that we saw around the area. In the meantime, on our Timeshare visit to Clearwater in Florida, we were invited by Ed and Shirley Weber, our old friends from Ohio, who had their winter home in a Gated Senior Community in Lakeland in Central Florida.

We fell in love with the place as soon as we entered the area and within three months became their neighbours!

As genetics is known to have a strong influence on Cardio-vascular disease, I was convinced that I would meet my Maker in the not too distant future as my father did. (He didn't survive the second heart attack a year after the first one). As we hardly knew anybody in that Community in Lakeland and our son being 1,000 miles away from there, we both felt that in the event of my sudden demise, Audrey would find it far less difficult to cope with in England than in Florida.

We therefore also bought a house in England near our daughter in a quiet cul-de-sac in Sutton Coldfield—a 400-year old town near Birmingham in the West Midlands. The idea was that we would spend the summer in England and winter in Florida. We did it for eight years until 2010, when instead of Audrey outliving me, I outlived her!

The light went out of my life!

Audrey passed away in England in the evening of 31 October 2010 within an hour from start to finish. Davinder our son-in-law and Shanta my daughter took charge of everything that needed to be done. Neil and Shomita arrived from the States as soon as they could.

But then I go too fast. She was gifted with some especial qualities that must be mentioned.

Soon after she wrote her brief autobiography, she got interested in Genealogy and enrolled on a website. I was somewhat surprised by her dedication. She must have spent thousands of hours in this pursuit. When she finally stopped, she had a family tree of 1,001 (yes 1,001) names of her ancestors.

In the pursuit she came in contact with two of her distant relations—a gentleman from Cheshire, England, and a lady from Canberra, Australia. They exchanged so many E-mails that they became quite close. We exchanged visits with Jack of Cheshire, and at our invitation Lynn from Australia spent a few days with us in Sutton Coldfield during her visit to England. They were very shocked by the news of her passing away and sent me their condolences.

The Company I used to work for in India had an In-house monthly magazine. It used to publish short stories, poems, reports of Company functions, etc., other than the Company News. During our stay in India, quite a few of her short stories and poems were published in various issues of the magazine. The Company had Manufacturing Divisions in different parts of India and hence the magazine had a wide circulation within the company. There were a few letters to the Editor commending her write-ups.

She also had the gift of composing poems to suit special occasions like friends' birthdays, anniversaries, weddings etc. She would write a poem in about an hour or so before we were to start out!

In Lakeland on the eve of the 80th birthday party of Robert Hoagland, one of our fellow residents, whose ancestors came from Holland, Audrey made a dress that an elderly Dutch lady of olden days would wear; Audrey made herself up to suit the dress and read out her poem (including some Dutch words) especially written to celebrate his 80th birthday in our Club House in front of a few hundred friends. That was the highlight of the party as it was quite a surprise for everybody especially for the Birthday Boy and with her sense of humour she brought the house down!

One of her qualities that I found out much later in our life together was compassion. Donating to charities is nothing unusual. Through Action Aid—a well-known Charity in the U.K.—she "adopted" a young girl from Africa back in the 80s and through Autopay arranged with our UK bank to send a regular amount. It is **still going on.**

Action Aid sent me a beautiful letter of condolence. I still get letters from the recipients with their pictures.

One particular example of her sense of care and love for my people comes to my mind.

Even after my nephews and niece grew up and settled down I carried on supporting my sister which I continued to do when we moved to the US. I thought one day that as they can well support their mother (my sister), perhaps I don't need to carry on sending her money. When I asked my nephews and niece, they wrote back that they can well look after their mother and hence I can stop supporting her, which I did. I hadn't discussed this with Audrey. When I did, she asked me the amount in American Dollars. When I told her (she knew that I sent her money but obviously didn't know the amount), she said that if it were herself, she wouldn't have stopped it since that was quite a small amount compared to our income. So I wrote to my sister that at Audrey's suggestion I am resuming the payment. My sister wrote us a beautiful letter and said that she couldn't stop crying when she received my letter! I carried on until 1994 when she had a massive stroke and went into a coma from which she never recovered.

She was only 56!

Another quality that she herself "discovered" was her power of imagination to write fiction. She wrote two historical novels and had intended to write a trilogy based on Battles. The day before she passed away she asked me to E-mail the Publisher to give the final go ahead for printing her second and last book titled *Naseby*, based on the civil war in England between Cromwell and King Charles I which changed the destiny of England. She wanted the book to be published before Christmas (of 2010). The publisher did publish it on time but the author had left the world by then!

I was very, very fortunate indeed that Audrey married me! I am also very blessed with my children, their lovely spouses and wonderful grandsons.

I now live with my memories of her for over 52 years including nearly 50 years as her husband! Having a loving family as I have is a blessing from God.

Chapter 3

Photographs

Audrey as a baby

Audrey as a girl

Audrey as a teenager with her Mum and Dad

Audrey with her University friends, Sheffield 1957

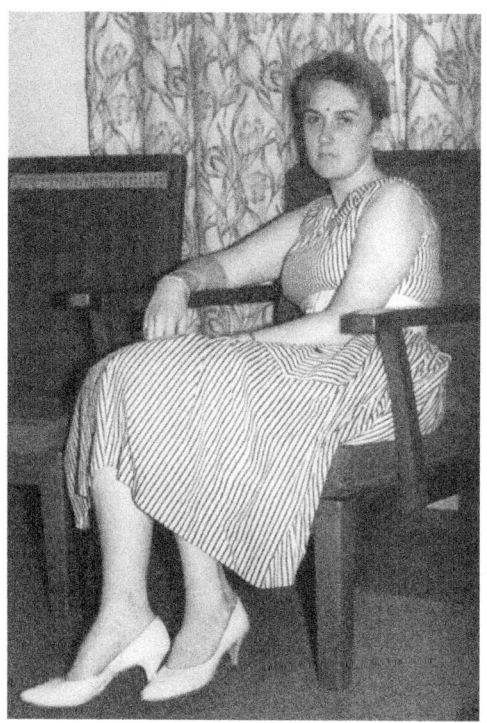

The first time Anu met Audrey, Sheffield 1959

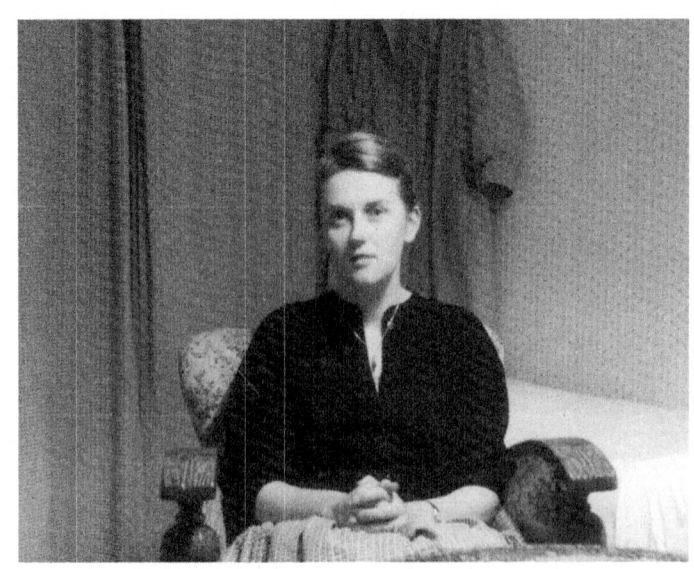

Audrey Amsterdam 1960

Wedding picture, Audrey, Anu, her Mum and Dad,
Bridesmaid Norma and Best Man Pravat, 6 May 1961

Wedding cake cutting

The Bride and Groom arrive in Calcutta airport, 10 May 1961

New born baby Shanta with Neil, Anu, Audrey & parents,
St Helens 1964

Audrey, Anu, Neil, Shanta, Anu's parents (Snehamay &
Kamala)and brother Santimoy, 1967

200

Audrey, Anu, Neil, Shanta, Anu's and Audrey's parents (Ernest & Zena) Thane, India 1971

Audrey with her mum and children, Marve Beach, Bombay, 1971

Audrey dancing at an Indian wedding reception

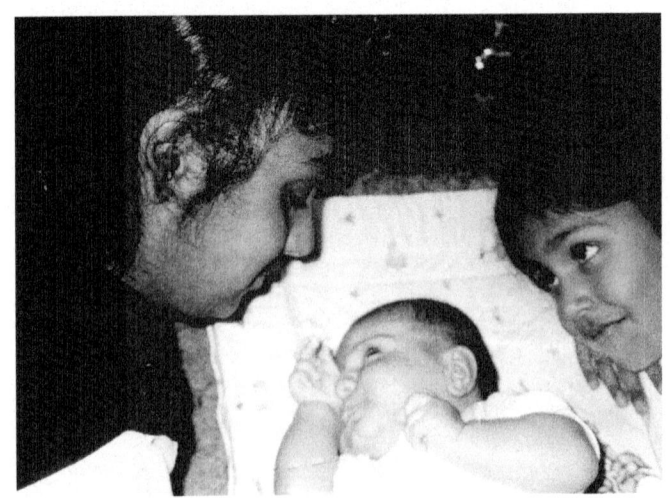

Shanta's 3 boys – Arjun, Amar & Harkrishan

Audrey with son Neil & daughter-in-law Shomita, Chicago 2000

Audrey & Anu holidaying in America

Audrey by her Christmas tree

Audrey with Neil, Chicago 1998

Audrey, Anu, Shanta, her family & friends, Orrville Ohio 1993

Audrey, Shanta, Neil, Dav and his mother Rattan,
Arjun & Amar

Audrey, Anu and his sister Renu, Madras 2003

Audrey with baby Harkrishan, Coventry 1998

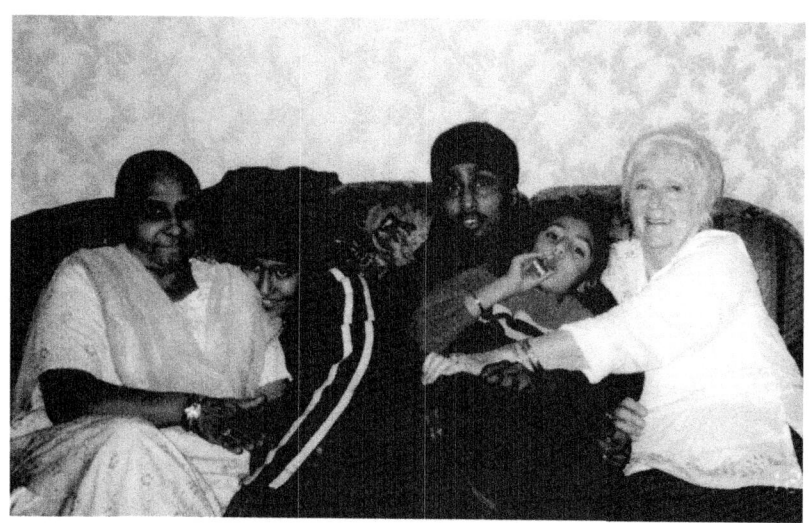

Audrey and Rattan with all their grandchildren, Coventry 2001

*Audrey and first grandson Arjun, Sutton Coldfield, England
2004*

Audrey and son Neil, Sutton Coldfield, England 2010

Audrey and son-in-law Dav, at her 70th birthday 2008

Audrey cuts cake

Audrey & Charlotte, our granddaughter-in-law, Lakeland,
Florida

Audrey with her first book (Talavera), Lakeland Florida

Printed in Great Britain
by Amazon

61517074R00122